The Teacher and His Philosophy

THE PROFESSIONAL EDUCATION SERIES

Walter K. Beggs, *Editor*
Dean Emeritus
Teachers College
University of Nebraska

Royce H. Knapp, *Research Editor*
Regents Professor of Education
Teachers College
University of Nebraska

The Teacher and His Philosophy

by

JOHN P. MARSHALL

Assistant Professor of Philosophy
Trinity University, San Antonio

PROFESSIONAL EDUCATORS PUBLICATIONS, INC.
LINCOLN, NEBRASKA

Library of Congress Catalog Card No.: 72-90382

ISBN   0-88224-027-7

Contents

The Case for Educational Philosophy

This book is directed to the student of teaching, whether he be in the process of learning the art and the craft in college, or whether he is a practicing teacher of some experience who desires to refine his artistry and improve his craftmanship. The purpose here is undergirded by the simple premise that neither the student in training nor the practicing professional can successfully achieve these objectives unless and until he is fairly sure of his own value orientation, the purposes and objectives that grow out of his values, and a set of criteria — anchored in something deeper than the convenience of the moment, or a simple hunch — with which to evaluate the progress and the success of his efforts. For, without such an anchor a teacher behaves merely as a mechanic who repairs a valve or replaces a component in a computer, without knowing or caring what the function of the valve or the component is or, if indeed, it has any function at all. The corollary in teaching would be the person who maintains contempt for "another dreary book about theory." "Who needs it?" he says, "if the theorist would only visit the schools and find out what needs doing, and come up with some specific answers, he would be more helpful. What we need are practices and formulas that help us to solve our problems."

We cannot quarrel with either the need for formulas or the need for direction in solving problems, but here again formulas and direction should be based on values, ideas, and tested conclusions more profound and sophisticated than the convenience, expedience, or the hunches growing out of a given situation.

This is what invites and encourages the great teacher to enter into the fascinating, wonderful, and useful world of philosophy. We use these rather elaborate adjectives deliberately because they all apply. We could also say that philosophy can be most complex and abstract, and highly theoretical — and philosophers? — well, they can be arranged from the ordinary person who thinks a little bit about what he feels is important, why things are as they are, the meaning of the minutiae of his environment, all of the way to the philosophical purist, who deals with abstract theory, and meanings and shadings of meanings, and incidentally, a vocabulary which only he and a few of his contemporaries understand.

Teaching and preparing for teaching are value oriented. Teachers, like all professionals, have learned that all people need and search for the meaning and values in their lives. Ever since the human species acquired the ability to think, man has attached some sort of meaning to his existence. It may be true that for many people this process is quite low-level and unsophisticated; often, not much more, to use a modern expression, than a "gut reaction" to what is happening to them and around them. But even this activity may become institutionalized and lead to firm convictions as to what is important or good; and conversely, to what is unimportant and undesirable, or even bad. From this process values are formed and habits of thinking and behaving are developed. People tend to group themselves around certain of these systems of needs, values, convictions, and desires or dislikes — into tribes, communities, clubs, political parties, religious dogmas, and a myriad of other combinations. Obviously, all of this can be most complex and interrelated, and very, very confusing, unless one — and here we use the phrase again — is anchored in some systematic way of thinking about the whole complex business.

For thousands of years scholars have pondered these matters. Some have chosen to chronicle the story of mankind's development. These are the historians. Others have studied institutions, communities, and organized social systems. These are sociologists. There are also economists, anthropologists, paleontologists, and political scientists, each claiming a segment of the panorama of human behavior for his disciplined study. But the scholar who endeavors to reduce the complete range of man's thought processes and the related behavior patterns into some sort of understandable categories is the philosopher. In this book we will not be concerned with the nuances and overtones, and the finely honed shadings of meanings which occupy and delight the pure philosopher. Rather, the hope is to help the teacher, potential or practicing, to root his own contemplation of himself, and what he is doing and why, into a reasonably analytical and comprehensive cumulative system of meaning.

Actually this is the stuff of teaching. No matter what the teaching specialty — history, English, mathematics, physical education, or typewriting—a rational design is always present. The teacher is dealing with a learner, who in his own turn is plagued with questions about himself and his worth, about the meaning of his experiences and the things that are happening to him and his immediate environment. The learner is always subject to a confusing array of forces and influences and requirements which bombard him from a dozen directions at the same time. These come from many sources—his home background, his community, his peer group, and particularly the school's expectations of him. Moreover, the learner's own desires, aspirations, and problems are always determinants of his motivation, interest, and achievements.

This is especially true in the United States, where the schools are a public trust and their activities are always a reflection of conflicting social values. What appears to some to be a lack of direction in our schools is not necessarily a weakness but fortunately mirrors the increasing pluralism and freedom of a multi-culture nation. Above everything else, teachers must resist the temptation to panic and be captured by some transitory proclamation or, even worse, by propaganda. The very least they can do is to attempt to understand the diverse needs and values of the society and make some conscious choices about what is acceptable and good for the learners and schools. Rather than to patch and make short-range comfortable decisions which may create dire, long-range consequences, time should be taken to analyze the current problems and ponder the solutions from the base of a carefully conceived educational philosophy. This is undoubtedly the most urgent need of the current educational scene, if the school program, or more especially a variety of programs, is to have a beneficial and viable impact on the growth of learners. Now let us consider educational philosophy, its nature and scope, and the contribution it can make to teachers.

The educational philosopher is, as the name implies, both a philosopher and an educator. Like the philosopher, he appraises man's attempts to bring order and regularity to his experiences in the world. He examines the culture of man and man-made systems of thought. He considers the material and non-material accomplishments and the total man-made environment: dams, machines, laws, books, liquor, religions, and works of art. As a philosopher, he seeks for meaning in human existence through a comprehensive and consistent analysis of basic questions: Who am I? What is the nature of man? What is truth? Why do we need societies? What can I hope? How ought I to live? Philosophy, then, is man's attempt to make an articulate and logical appraisal about the meaning, value, and continuity of life. As these questions are explored and reexamined, the student of philosophy tends to become more consistent and reliable; he is becoming a "philosopher" when he asks "Where does this latest knowledge fit?"

As an educator, the philosopher of education attempts to develop a logical and consistent framework through which the educative process may be fruitfully viewed; but educational philosophy cannot be completely separated from "pure" philosophy, since it is concerned with most of the same questions in a somewhat different context.

Nor can educational philosophy be considered totally apart from the history of education, the sociology of education, comparative education, psychology and measurements, or educational administration. The educational philosopher attempts to synthesize such more or less specialized parts into a unified whole. The educational philosopher asks all teachers and laymen to join him in pondering whether the purpose of our schools is to preserve all of our cultural heritage, some, or none. Together these parties, each at his own level, debate whether the schools should preserve our society as it is or work for social change through the schools. If it is decided that the school is both the bearer of custom, heritage, and tradition, and the agency for turning away from the bondage of the past, the problems, of necessity, multiply. On the other hand, if the past is ignored, the question emerges, how do we determine and justify the directions we choose?

These are some of the fundamental questions around which the great educational minds of the past have built their thinking and evolved their philosophies, and these philosophies are worthy of our own careful study and contemplation. They illustrate the best thinking on the major problems of education; the answers others have found may help us to understand our problems or at the very least to discover that ours are not necessarily unique. The philosophies, furthermore, are of value because they lead us to consider education in a consistent way through a particular philosophical framework or perhaps even from less profound patterns which exist in another form in our folk wisdom, religion, and art. They help us to clarify and express our own thoughts about education; if we don't find the "right" answer, at least we will know how to ask the "right" kinds of questions. And, finally they help us to formulate our own philosophical perspectives by which we can view the total educational program and from which we can take what we hope is intelligent action.

As noted previously, every teacher functions in a complex situation. He works directly with learners who differ in many ways. Each is a unique bundle of abilities, in part inherited and in part learned. Each comes to school with a unique social experience—in his home and family, among his peers, in his community, and from his society generally. He has some ideas of what is important for him, and so do his parents and his friends and the people of his community. He is also in a school which subjects him to another set of generally formalized expectations—a curriculum designed to help him get more knowledge, sharpen his skills, improve his thinking—in short to grow and develop into a mature person.

As the teacher makes his own contribution to this growth pattern, he must operate within and through the maze of forces and influences that are playing on and shaping the learner from other directions. In one sense the teacher is a middleman. He stands between the homespun value systems of the community where he works, and the incredible panorama of mankind's intellectual experience over the years, and it is his unique responsibility to bring the past and the present into some sort of blend, a synthesis that is understandable and meaningful to the learners under his charge.

We have already pointed out that the experiences out of history have been formalized into schools or systems of thinking about education and its problems and that it is incumbent on every teacher at least to know what these systems are and to use them in shaping his own orientation. Obviously, scholars over the years have differed in their conclusions, so there are a number of divisions or categories to be considered, and these can be classified in different ways. For our purposes here, however, we have arbitrarily chosen five to be outlined in some depth: Idealism, Realism, Perennialism, Pragmatism, Existentialism. The reader will note that there are overlaps at certain points but that each has a definite focus. There are also adherents to each point of view, some of whom are almost fanatical in their devotion. Others, on the contrary, find that deep adherence to any one position is much too confining and that it is possible to discover points of agreement with two or more, or even all of them. This process of picking and choosing from a number of premises is called eclecticism, which, in effect, is a philosophy in its own right, although some purists might probably brand it a form of anti-intellectualism.

For the reader it is perhaps best to remain in a relatively eclectic position for a time, until the essentials of the five philosophies defined in the following pages are fairly well digested and understood. Each system will be described in some detail with enough of its history traced to give it continuity, and relate it to the classic subdivision of philosophy, namely: metaphysics, epistemology, axiology, ethics, aesthetics, and logic. Since these terms appear frequently the following definitions should be helpful:

By *metaphysics* we mean the description of the nature of trans-empirical reality and the different levels of being within it.

By *epistemology*, we mean the method we use to weigh the evidence of the external world.

By *axiology* we mean the study of the basis for the value standards applied in ethics, aesthetics, religion, and art.

By *aesthetics*, we mean the study of what beauty is and how we come to define and value it.

By *logic*, we mean those formal checks on inquiry which determine the consistency and reasonableness of argument based on what we admit as evidence.

Additional terms will be defined as needed in the context of the following chapters.

SUGGESTED READINGS

BECK, LEWIS WHITE. *Philosophic Inquiry: An Introduction to Philosophy.* Englewood Cliffs, N.J.: Prentice-Hall, 1959. This time-tested text is remarkably comprehensive and distinguishes clearly between the analytic and speculative functions of philosophy.

BRINTON, CRANE. *Ideas and Men: The Story of Western Thought.* New York: Prentice-Hall, 1950. This is an extremely readable and comprehensive history of Western culture. It provides the historic frame needed for the meaningful study of any philosophy. With remarkable precision it shows how ideas from the worlds of science and art are reflected in past philosophies.

DEWEY, ROBERT E., FRANCIS W. GRAMLICH, and DONALD LOFTSGORDON. *Problems of Ethics.* New York: Macmillan, 1961. This book is a fine collection of essays about the rankings of ways of viewing ethical values. The selections reflect the history of philosophy and dramatize how questions about ethics constantly recur.

DURANT, WILL. *The Pleasure of Philosophy.* New York: Simon & Schuster, 1953. This amazing and enjoyable book, which makes philosophy come alive for the non-technical philosopher, was originally published as *The Mansions of Philosophy.* Durant is readable and has an uncanny ability to make of the study of philosophy a joy and a passion.

KNELLER, GEORGE F. (ed.). *Foundations of Education.* New York: John Wiley, 1963. This outstanding text for the study of the intellectual and cultural foundations of education is concerned with the range of problems which education has confronted and must confront. It is remarkably comprehensive.

PARK, JOE (ed.). *Selected Readings in the Philosophy of Education*. New York: Macmillan, 1968. The fine introduction to the various philosophies and selections from writers past and present who represent the different schools of thought provides broad perspectives for considering educational problems. A great value of the book is its fairness to all points of view.

RANDALL, JOHN HERMAN, JR., and JUSTUS BUCHLER. *Philosophy, an Introduction*. New York: Barnes & Noble; College Outline Series, No. 41, 1942. This paperback is a rich source for understanding the categories and vocabulary of philosophy. It is extremely readable and comprehensive.

SAHAKIAN, WILLIAM S. *Systems of Ethics and Value Theory*. Patterson, N.J.: Littlefield, Adams, 1964. This sound paperback in the New Student Outline Series provides a comprehensive guide to readings in value theory. The book has the value of extensive quotations from primary sources and excellent bibliographies for each of the authors discussed.

THILLY, FRANK, and LEDGER WOOD. *A History of Philosophy*. New York: Henry Holt, 1958. As the title implies, the book is historically organized and directed to the cultural context in which ideas have developed. Though academic, the book is very readable and makes cross-referencing between authors possible.

CHAPTER 1

Idealism

The term "idealism" is more consistently used in educational philosophy than it is in "pure" academic philosophy, where the history of the word shows it to have meant different, sometimes opposing, things at different times. What it never means in either is our common-sense notion of high-minded striving for excellence: that is, "He was very idealistic." Closer to the mark is the notion that some concepts like "truth, beauty, and honor," are absolute; they are the famous "eternal verities." They will always remain undiluted as "ideals" and can never be watered down or redefined or negated even if we never experience or embody them. They are universal — permanent — in that their definition remains constant for all times and places regardless of the secular history of any civilization or epoch. These ideals are thought to be more important and basic than any factual knowledge of the world. As objects of contemplation these first principles of a spiritual nature are "metaphysical" — beyond, independent of, and superior to any description of the world. Such concepts are *a priori:* They always exist prior to and separate from the world of experience. Their ontological status, value-priority, though not demonstrable by science, is more important than life itself; they are "worth" more than the sum total of any man's accomplishments in life and worth any sacrifice: that is, "Socrates died for *truth.*" "Jesus was crucified so that *Love* for man could live." In viewing the universe, the idealists see ideals as being more real, more permanent, and more valuable than any set of events; such ideals are "better" than the physical world or anything that happens in it; they are metaphysical — spiritual essences. Their status in cosmology — our picture of the priority of values in the structure of the universe — is more constant and important than all of the successes or failures, as they are secularly defined, in the lives of any number of men in the world.

14

Idealism holds that little lives and total existences are nothing compared to the beauty and truth of these magnificent ideals which we strive to attain and which guide our conduct in life. They have the status of moral laws for rational beings because they guide our behavior regardless of circumstance or consequence; they are of greater significance as guides to action than any trivial, physical law about, say, gravity or motion. They are the higher laws which induce an Antigone or a Jesus or a Jefferson to rebel against the man-made laws of a particular society when these laws ignore or fall short of the realization of some "higher truth" or "higher order." Idealism, then, sees the truth of ideals to be immutable, permanent, and unchanging; as a philosophical position it adheres to the view that nothing of value exists except as it is an idea in the mind of man, the mind of God, or in some super- or supra-natural realm. Such essences can never be discovered, confirmed, or rejected by our science or our sense perception; they are objectively most real to the idealist.

Notice the emphasis on mind. It is man as the embodiment of reason whose rationalism, speculative intelligence, enables him to grasp the ultimate realities (the *real* world) beyond, above, and superior to the mundane, factual world of impressions and illusions. In order, then, to know something of the Real world (the realm of Ideas and Ideals) we must withdraw from the use of our senses and the distracting frenzy of the practical world of consuming and producing, spending, and earning. In a sense, the idealists are aristocrats whose leisure is used for a noble purpose. This use of our intellects alone and disregard of the information of the senses is purely rational. When we use such a purely intellectual method, we are rationalists; we are guided in the world by the philosophical theory of *rationalism*. To the idealist, the universe is of the nature of mind. It is an idea. This indicates that the real nature of the position is idea-ism. The universe for the idealist has two aspects. The first is the sensory aspect: that part of life open to empirical or sensory exploration and verification. This is a sham world: a world of illusion. The Real world lies beyond this and can only be reached through the intellect. This is the world of Ideas.

As we would expect, the idealist takes a rationalistic approach to the knotty problems of knowledge and truth, and relies heavily on deductive logic (the process of reasoning from the truth of some general assumption to a specific conclusion). To use an example from the truth of a Christian dogma:

(Major premise) All men are fallen creatures (sinners).
(Minor premise) (All) John Doe is a man.

Conclusion: John Doe is a fallen creature (sinner).

Note that in this standard form of deductive argument, the syllogism, the conclusion must be valid if the major premise is true. We have no choice but to agree with the conclusion, since the logic of rationalism does not require us to prove our primary assertions; and our only checks on method are the rules of deductive logic, which show how the validity of the relationships stated in the conclusion came about. Of course it is possible to have a "true" first premise supported by science.

All dogs are mammals.
Fido is a dog.

Fido is a mammal.

In this case, the answer is most desirable — true and valid. The point is that the rationalist equates logical validity with truth, even if the conclusion is contrary to all our knowledge. To paraphrase the dictum of Socrates, "The unexamined life is not worth living," we could say "the unexamined or untestable major premise is not worth following." Everything the rationalistic philosophers tell us may be valid; but it does not follow that anything they say is true. It can be charged that they tell us "all about everything and nothing about anything." For a drastic example,

All baboons are lollipops (the reverse is no more true)
King is a baboon

King is a lollipop.

In this case, nothing is true except the minor premise, but the conclusion is still *valid.* It is possible, then, as the moderns agree, that grand speculative systems of rationism which depend upon deductive logic might all be valid but false. Even so, most idealists hold to the coherence theory of truth, which is an epistemological theory which holds that truth exists when a proposition is part of a system of propositions or is consistent with a body of propositions (an established dogma). For a crude example, we could say that a note on a piano is in tune only when it is in tune to the other notes on the same piano. No note is in tune simply to itself. Of course, the notes on a piano may be in tune to one another—all flat or sharp—without being in tune to any other piano.

Although some idealist thinkers have carefully denied reliance on empirical or sense data, such data usually serves as the basis for the premises of deductive logic. The idealist attempts to find, in the universe, general principles which can be given the status of Universal Truths. As we discover these Truths or Ideas we acquire real knowledge. One way of doing this is by looking at ourselves and the world as representations of Absolute Self and the Absolute Universe. It is assumed that since Truth does exist, and is not merely a creation of the individual or the society, it can be found, and when it is found it will be absolute and binding. In ethics, the best form of conduct is to live guided by the ideals. For the idealist the good life is living in harmony with the universe. If the Absolute is viewed as the final and most ethical of all things and persons, or as God, who is, by definition, perfect and is thus perfect in morals, the idealist epitome of ethical conduct and morality will lie in the imitation of Absolute Self. Man is most moral when his behavior is in accord with the Ideal and Universal Moral Law which we can and do recognize. We do right simply because it is right (Kant's Categorical Imperative). It is indeed a lofty ideal of morality that implies we do right simply to be more perfectly in tune with the universe. To some, it means being in accordance with God's plan. That is, we try to live up to some supernatural plan; for the idealists argue that we can never discover how we "ought" to live by describing how men do live.

In aesthetics—what is beauty—the idealist is also true to his forms. The idealist sees as beautiful the approximation of the Ideal. That which finitely attempts to express the Absolute is categorized as aesthetically pleasing. When we enjoy a work of art it is because, on the one hand, we see it as a true representation of the Ideal; and on the other hand, it serves to bring us closer to contact with the Ideal. Music is considered by some idealists as the highest form of aesthetic creation, since it does not represent anything in the phenomenal or existent world, but cuts across it to the heart of the Absolute. The artist should, according to this school of thought, attempt to idealize the world to us, that is to portray its inner meaning rather than to represent it as it appears to the senses—capture its inner essence, its oneness with the Ideal. Art is, by this view, inspirational rather than photographic.

For a clearer view of the social and educational consequences of consistent idealism, we would do well to consider the first systematic example of it in Plato's *Republic*. Plato distinguishes between the use of reason and the use of the senses. His position is that in order to know something of the real world (the realm of Ideas) we must withdraw from the use of our senses and rely on a purely intellectual approach. This use of reason or the intellect alone is usually referred to by the technical name of *rationalism*.

As we would expect, Plato's parable or "myth of the cave" presents us with one who escapes from the shadows and echos of the cave and those still in the cave who worship them as real. When he returns from the bright, outside world and attempts to tell others of its wonders and their plight, they refuse to believe his glorious vision. Plato may see in his metaphorical description the rejection of Socrates and his martyrdom at the hands of the "cave dwellers" of Athens.

Plato therefore rejects democracy in favor of the leadership of the wisest and the best who do not perceive the world as shifting, deceptive shadows or distorting echos. Those managers, government experts, and rulers who perceive the real behind the facade of appearances and common sense are like the world controller in Aldous Huxley's *Brave New World;* they are the "fascist" leaders who legislate how other lesser people should live and what they should believe. Since the average man could not and would not understand the rational concepts which underlie experience, he is not told of them by the "philosopher-king," enlightened despot, who rules.

In the *Republic,* those unselfish thinkers closest to the essence of such concepts are most important. The ruling class perpetuates itself and its ideal for society through education. The least perfect of men are trained as artisans and workmen, since they — like artists generally — merely copy the physical forms and shapes of the shifting world. Only the philosopher-king and his trusted assistants realize the triviality of the lives of the great mass of men. The practicality and short-sightedness of the selfish eliminates them from further education. Until quite recently, eliminations of the mass of men from even college preparatory courses were a part of much of the European system of education. In the *Republic,* note the disdain of the rulers for the average man and how "doers" are thought to be of a lesser order than thinkers. Such a caste system makes the great bulk of the citizenry a kind of slave class which supports, much like the wide base of a pyramid, the goals and ends of those above them in the social and intellectual classes. For their own good, the mass of men are deceived by "big lies" into conformity with ends they could not comprehend. Yet the mass of producers and consumers are so well controlled that they are happy doing what they must and are easily deceived into thinking that their trivial lives have meaning and are the result of freely chosen direction.

Those students perceptive enough to comprehend the glimmerings of "Reality" are given further education. A second major class is the military. Though the working citizenry may think the military protects them, the military may be as necessary to the bureaucratic rulers as a protection against the citizenry. If it were necessary in the eyes of the rulers, the military would comply, since they have more of the "big picture" and have been taught more of the "real truth" than the rest of the populace, who are inferior to them.

For the ultimate good of society, the most important persons to be trained through education are those who will enter the governmental bureaucracy as part of the apex of the pyramid. Even some future philosopher-king-ruler will be trained for as much as fifty years to assume the pinnacle of power. For those who join the ruling class the aim of education is to take the child through the history of the race so that he may reflect the Truth of the ages, which is knowledge of the Absolute. The aims of the idealist are centered on the conception of Ultimate Reality and the idea that the Ideal really exists and can be known, at least in part, by man. The pupil is a spiritual being in the process of becoming. He is, in a sense, a small representation of the Absolute Self. The student must bring himself closer to the Absolute through imitation of the exemplar (the teacher) and through study of those subjects (the humanities) which best represent or symbolize the true ideas of which the human race has knowledge.

The idealist sees the teacher as having perhaps the most important single role in the educative process. It is the teacher who serves the student as a living exemplar of what the student can become. The teacher should set an example that the student will follow. This is, of course, compatible with the notion that the real world (the world of the senses) is an imperfect copy of the Absolute. Thus, the closer we are to come to the Absolute, the more we must model our behavior upon those persons that we know are paradigm cases. Some moderns would say this is authoritarianism.

The subject matter for the school is that which is concerned with Ideal man and Ideal society. Books are the sources of this subject matter—the subject matter of ideas. Thus, to understand society and life we must study history. To understand man we must study literature and the humanities. The idealist wants to see the entire and absolute pattern of life; and for this, history and the humanities are the most important subjects. The idealist tradition of subject matter is basically literary and places its primary emphasis on the subject matter of books, and especially those literary pieces considered the masterworks of humanity. Books, not the subject matter of experience, are the sources of information about ideas. The idealist has little use for field trips and empirical or sensory data.

The idealist method tends to be based on lecture and discussion. It is primarily a system of training by discussion for the handling of ideas absorbed from the lectures. The student also learns through the method of imitation. The imitation may be of his teacher or of some other person, real or literary, who is closely attuned to the Absolute. Thus, the idealist in his educational method relies on imitation, lecture, and discussion. All three are related to ideas that are already known and there is little or no opportunity for exploration of new areas of interest. Because of this there is a tendency to reinforce the cultural lag between education and the society. Moderns might call this indoctrination rather than education.

Not surprisingly, such a long period of internship for those who will become human technicians and supervisors tends to make them defenders of the "status quo." They are the orthodox whose faithful conformity to what they were taught makes them the natural leaders who are fit to become carbon copies of the authorities they replace. Indeed, such a system is often static and authoritarian. Its adherence to the past renders it suspicious of change or reform.

Cynics have suggested that such a system was implemented by the medieval church and many times since by those who claimed to rule by divine right. Bishop Berkeley is generally considered the father of modern idealism. He argues that what we experience, this book for example, does exist in a real physical sense only when someone is thinking of it. Otherwise it or any other object does not exist. It only exists when we perceive it in our minds; it is only then that this book really exists. The only place it exists permanently is in the Supreme Mind, which is always conscious of it. Berkeley avoids the problem of things winking in and out of existence as they are or are not thought of and allows for the continuity of existence by making the uniformities we experience in the universe the product of God's thoughts. Were it not for our minds when we use them to read this book, and the mind of God as a kind of storage bin when we are not contemplating it, this book would disappear; it only exists when God allows us to perceive it, since matter, like all reality, is essentially mental. The extreme of this position is called solipsism, which denies the existence of matter; the consistent solipsist would say that only the mind and ideals are real; other things exist only as mental states, since material substances are not real and the world of cabbages and kings only exists when we choose to perceive them with our minds — where they have their ultimate and only existence.

In Germany, Hegel formulated a dialectic logic which many have thought harnesses the ideals and brings them closer to realization as the world progresses; needless to say, this idealistic logic was denied by the materialist Marx, who still kept the dialectic. Neither an idealistic nor a materialistic dialectic can be supported by other systems of logic. Ironically, those who followed Marx to Utopia reentered a Platonic Republic complete with philosopher-kings where, as Orwell suggests in *Animal Farm* some pigs are more equal than others. Hegel's position is that nothing is real except the whole which he imagined to be embodied in the completely evolved Prussian state of his own time. Since the whole is greater than the parts, the state is greater than the sum total of its members, who exist only to serve it. He wrote that "The State Is the Marching God in the World." It can be argued that he and the authoritarian Martin Luther, not Nietzsche, are the fathers of modern fascism. The universe is seen as one evolving spiritual unity. This position is generally referred to as objective, or absolute, idealism. Within this system the universe is evolving through a dialectic process. This process begins with a statement called a thesis. Every thesis must have its opposite, or antithesis. As these two are reconciled, a synthesis emerges, which in turn becomes a new thesis. As man uses this dialectic process, he copies the world process. Hegel applied his theory to the study of history, viewing it as the continuous unfolding of the dialectic process. Most noticeably the fullest recent statement of the educational role of the philosophy of idealism can be gained by studying the educational system of Italy as it was reformed by Giovanni Gentile from 1922 to 1924. Gentile also developed a theoretical justification for fascism and the conception of man's subservient relationship to the state.

Perhaps, the most important figure in the American tradition of idealism was William Torrey Harris. A teacher of shorthand, Harris rose to be Superintendent of Schools in St. Louis, Missouri, and United States Commissioner of Education. The form of the absolute idealism of Harris was ardently Hegelian. His philosophic influence extended to a great many thinkers of the day. Among those influenced was the young American philosopher John Dewey. Harris founded and served as editor of the *Journal of Speculative Philosophy* and was, perhaps, the foremost American exponent for Hegelian idealism. Though Josiah Royce of Harvard was never associated with the St.

Louis movement, he was a Neo-Hegelian who had restated idealism so that the Absolute was viewed as a finished, closed system. Two of his more important disciples were William E. Hocking and Herman H. Horne, with whom the philosophy of idealism is generally linked in the United States. Perhaps the most sympathetic and kindly picture of contemporary idealism as it affects the problems of education is J. Donald Butler.

One of the major criticisms of idealism has been that it lacks an adequate social policy. The ideal society is seen as a reflection of the ideal organization of the Absolute. Society is like an organism in which each person (like the cells of the organism) has a particular place and role. The idealist relies for his social views on the accumulated wisdom of the past. Particularly that wisdom which is either symbolic of, or representative of, the Ideal. In general, therefore, the idealist stresses an intellectual pattern for conservation of the cultural heritage. This is a conservative position, typical of any system based on the belief that reality has a coercive order of its own and that we must wait to progress until we have this order made clear to us. Also, since the ideals do not change, there is no need for innovation or curricular reform.

Though the consistent idealist is quite likely to be an elitist and anti-democratic, the Western tradition and its religious heritage are extremely sympathetic to the "pull of ideals" as a pattern for emulation. We should, perhaps, wonder if the complexity and scope of modern government, education, and industry isn't creating a new class of specialized professional managers and planners more committed to their theories than their applicability or their adverse effects upon those they were designed to aid.

SUGGESTED READINGS

BARRETT, CLIFFORD. *Contemporary Idealism in America*. New York: Macmillan, 1932. This book shows the influence of idealism on American thought and life. It is not specifically concerned with educational problems.

BUTLER, J. DONALD. *Idealism in Education*. New York: Harper & Row, 1966, Butler's book is a comprehensive review of the history, rationale, and strengths and weaknesses of idealism as it affects education. Butler is a sympathetic spokesman for the view.

DUPUIS, ADRIAN M. *Philosophy of Education in Historical Perspective*. Chicago: Rand McNally, 1964. This book is of value in comparing the conceptual frameworks through which educational philosophies are viewed.

DURANT, WILL. *The Story of Civilization,* Volume 2: *The Life of Greece.* New York: Simon & Schuster, 1939. Durant's book is a magnificent view of the Greek world. It provides five sections on the formal thought, daily lives, and education of the civilization.

LAMPRECHT, STERLING. *Our Philosophical Traditions.* New York: Appleton-Century-Crofts, 1955. This is a first-rate introduction to idealistic thinkers throughout the ages. The book is also of immense value when studying other forms of philosophy.

MOURANT, JOHN A., and HANS FREUND. *Problems of Philosophy, a Book of Readings.* New York: Macmillan, 1964. This book is helpful in clarifying how the idealist comes to his epistemology. It has further value in the range of problems it discusses relevant to all the philosophies of education.

PLATO. *The Dialogues,* Four Volumes. Trans. by B. Jowett. New York: Charles Scribner, 1872. Many recent translations of sections of the Platonic Dialogues are readily available in paperback. Plato remains the prototype of the idealist.

_____. *The Republic.* Dozens of editions of this classic portrayal of how an idealistic philosophy could be implemented to govern a Utopian society are readily available. For contrast, one could follow *The Republic* with *1984* by George Orwell, *Brave New World* by Aldous Huxley, or *Walden Two* by B. F. Skinner.

WARNER, REX. *The Greek Philosophers.* New York: Mentor Books MP442, 1964. Warner's book is extremely helpful for those wishing to understand why the Greeks asked the kinds of questions they did and came to their own kinds of answers. The book has the further virtue of showing the differences between the thinking of the Greek thinkers.

CHAPTER 2

Realism

Though it is possible to consider idealism and realism together in educational philosophy under the heading of essentialism, this grouping is misleading and may confuse more than illuminate. Those who hold these views of the nature of truth are similar in that they view it as immutable, permanent, and unchanging. Both tend to be deontological systems which speculate about how we "ought" to conduct our lives. Morality, then, is to be weighed against a metaphysical standard; consequently, the righteousness of an act is determined by one's attempt to live up to some predetermined higher moral law rather than for any selfish reason. In both cases, the essence of such laws precedes our existence. If our intention is good and our motives are pure, the consequences of our acts are of no importance. Most Christians are probably most aware of this position as a vital force through their religious training, which teaches them of the absolute value of such concepts as charity, compassion, and humility.

Yet the view of the universe held by the realist and the idealist is so radically different that they deserve separate discussion. Whereas the idealist philosophers have traditionally concerned themselves with "pure" philosophy and particularly with the ontological aspects of "pure" philosophy, the realists have been deeply concerned with the problems of epistemology. Most importantly, realism has come to be a philosophical position that holds to the view that reality, this book for example, is totally independent of any knowledge of it, where an idealist would say that a tree in the middle of the desert exists only if it is in some mind, or if there is some knowledge of it. The realist would hold that whether or not anyone or anything is thinking about the tree, it nevertheless exists. The realist has revolted against the notion that things that are experienced are dependent upon a knower for their existence. Though such a view may be more comforting to our common sense it creates as many problems for philosophy as it solves.

24

For the realist, ontology and metaphysics are still necessary. The universe is composed of matter in motion. It is the physical world in which we live that makes up reality. We can, on the basis of our experiences, recognize certain regularities in it which we generalize about and call laws. The vast cosmos rolls on despite man. Matter continues in motion whether man concerns himself with it or not. It is not unlike a giant machine in which man is both participant and spectator. This machine not only involves the physical universe, it operates in the moral, social, and economic spheres as well. The realist sees the immutable laws governing man's behavior as part of the machine — they are natural laws. The realist may be a monist, believing in one substance, a dualist, believing in two, or a pluralist, believing in many. Whichever he is though, he believes that all substances have a real existential status independent of the observer. He sees the world as having an orderly nature and composition which exists independent of consciousness, but which man may, and has, come to know a great deal about.

Here the similarities between different groups of realists diverge, as we might expect of proponents of any system of thought with a 2,500-year history. Although some of the early pre-Socratic thinkers dealt with the problems of the physical world and attempted to reduce the diversity of the world to some basic substance like fire or water, the first detailed realistic position is generally attributed to Aristotle. His statement of the system of realism is usually called classical realism.

Aristotle had been a student of Plato's and much of his thinking was either an attempt to come to terms with Plato's idealism in an empirical universe or a reaction to Plato's realm of Ideas. Aristotle distinguished reality into form and matter. Matter is the substance that all things have in common. Form is what distinguishes them. Yet form is, to this view, inherent in matter just as the oak tree is contained in the acorn and the man is contained in the infant: There are no other options.

For Aristotle these two categories were logically separable, although always found together in the empirical world. The more closely anything approaches pure form, the higher it is in the Aristotelian hierarchy. At the top of this hierarchy is pure form, which may be viewed as the highest form of reason. It is the Prime Mover which gives the universe its orderly nature. Matter, which is at the base of hierarchy, is nothing by itself. Closest to the bottom of the hierarchy are such things as earth and stones. Farther up the scale comes man, the heavens, and finally the Prime Mover, which is pure form and reason. Christians would call this uncaused cause "God," or the "Unmoved Mover."

Yet we should realize that realism is more than a modification of idealism to allow for a more scientific study of the world of man. It is a separate, but equally absolute closed system; it is closed in the sense that it too operates in accordance with its own, different metaphysical, axiological, and epistemological presuppositions and attempts to account for and explain everything that happens in the universe: it gives reasons which are consistent in theory, but may or may not correspond to "reality." This attempt to build a philosophy which takes greater account of the rude and troubling "facts of life" than idealism so that theory and fact are mutually reinforcing and correspond is based more than idealism not only upon the coherence theory of truth which they share, but also upon the fruitful hypothesis of a correspondence theory of truth. By this theory, a statement (proposition like water boils at 20 degrees) is true if and only if its terms (words designating objects) correspond with known facts—evidence. The realist says a thing is true if our own judgments agree with the facts, laws, and principles of the objective world. Here we have the kernel of a rudimentary science.

Certainly, even the crudest science—even mythology, magic, or organized religion—attempts to show why and how the agonies of even a Job can be explained; that is, some attempt is made to show how the cause of Job's misfortunes determines the effects he suffered. Further, the attempt is made to explain away the cruel fact of Job's losses and justify them by reference to laws and principles which are thought to be equally "real" descriptions of the objective world. Certainly, to minimize the brute fact of Job's anguish it is as necessary for the realists as for the idealists to explain how it is the inevitable and just consequence of some determining principle that explains how the fact—reality—is to be understood, perhaps explained away. Yet the realist, like the idealist, attempts to explain how what happens is part of a general plan and not an isolated, unique incident to be taken at gruesome face value. By the same reasoning, the assassination of a young, peace-making statesman or the death of an infant, or the collapse of the Bridge of San Luis Rey, can be explained away and uplifting consolations provided for the victim's survivors. Here, we have the awkward crux of realism: it is not realistic! We can say justly, "Whose reality?" The contemporary apostles of "telling it like it is" would be at one anothers' throats in ten minutes because they mistake their particular experiences for what is supposed to be equally real for others, and they could not agree about "how it is." Of all the possible causes we can assign to behavior, "Which is true?" Further, will the same cause — say, an induction notice — produce the same effects in the draftees?

Even if we grant that there may be scientific laws which are more than convenient generalizations, how do we assess the relationship among those principles by which we organize our experience and attempt to gain a degree of regularity and predictability without carefully answering how it is we come to know the real world — an epistemological question. Even if we agree that water boils or freezes at certain temperatures when measured by accurate (truthful) instruments, the moral laws which supposedly control our behavior do not so neatly arrange themselves as iron filings attracted by a magnet. The laws of science describe; they do not prescribe. The "Moral Laws" prescribe without describing anything.

Such a rift has always been a part of the dilemma faced by the realist, perhaps never more than now. We can use the logical method of induction by which we measure when water will freeze; students can indeed by patient observation and controlled experiments discover that water has always frozen at a given temperature and probably will in the future. From particular experiences we, as students, can and do literally discover the physical laws of nature. This form of reasoning does not rely for the conclusions reached upon authority, only the "facts." This form of logic, called induction, reaches conclusions and generalizations only after an investigation of as many of the facts as possible or necessary. Such conclusions are reached after experience; they are therefore *a posteriori*. They are real because they agree with the known facts — evidence.

But what are the known facts about the so-called moral laws? When we say "Jesus wants me for a Sunbeam" is a fact, we cannot prove it by induction. Neither can we explain what we really ought to do with our lives without disagreeing with others about what life "really" is or means. The history of realism, then, is the chronicle of a battle fought by opposing armies claiming equally to be fighting for what is "really" the "real" way to view the "real" problems "realistically." The culmination of realism may well be pragmatism — though the pragmatists would deny it as emphatically as an angelic child caught with ten too many fingers in the cookie jar. These "realists" are ideologically motivated and there seems to be little basis for supposing that the peoples of North and South Vietnam or Northern and Southern Ireland will ever "really" agree about what "really" is or "really" should be done short of killing those who disagree with one camp or the other in the name of what is "really true." Nor is it easy to assess which side is really being "rational," if either.

As we have shown, there is a great likelihood that some realists will say there is only one order of "reality" — say the results of method of science; this is monism: everything can be explained in the same way using the same method. Some realists will be dualists, who claim there are two separate, distinct levels of reality which cannot be reduced to each other or explain each other. Typical dualisms are mind-matter, mind-heart, spirit-matter, or mind-soul. Some realists may even be pluralists who believe, as the early Greeks and other polytheists, that every emotion, mind state, or basic part of nature like the seas, heavens, or woods requires its own set of explanations — god, goddesses, or both. How many moderns are pluralists who change values more easily than clothes as they move from home to business to church?

Despite the many forms it can take, the philosophy of realism has had a number of educational spokesmen through the centuries. Among the realists there have been a number of great educational spokesmen. Among these educators were John Amos Comenius, John Locke, Johann Herbart, Fredrick S. Breed, and Harry S. Broudy.

In the history of realism in the seventeenth and eighteenth centuries, Comenius and Locke stand out. John Amos Comenius, a Moravian bishop, was an advocate of a position known as Sense Realism. Much of his writing, including *The Great Didactic*, was in the realm of education. His *Orbis Pictus* was the first successful textbook which set out to appeal to the senses through the use of pictures. Comenius felt that the human mind, like a mirror, reflected everything around it. This view of mind makes man a spectator of the world rather than a participant.

John Locke is generally associated with the notion of mind as *tabula rasa*, or the mind as a blank sheet on which the outside world must leave its impressions. This view of mind was not new with Locke. In essence, it says that man is born with neither ready-made ideas nor with ideas which lie dormant in the mind. Man is born without innate ideas. At the time of birth, man's mind is a blank slate, upon which sensory experience of the world creates impressions. These impressions or experiences are of primary and secondary qualities. The primary qualities, such as extension in space, solidity, position, and motion, are the true characteristics of physical objects. Every object shows all the primary attributes in some degree. The secondary qualities are attributes of a sensory nature — taste, touch, smell, etc. — and it is not necessary that an object have all of these. We know about the attributes of things through ideas in our mind that come through sense observation or reflection.

In the history of realism in the nineteenth century, Herbart domin-
ates. Johann Herbart was more concerned with education than with
philosophy, although he held the chair of philosophy at Königsberg,
once held by Kant, and lectured in philosophy as well as education.
Herbart held that we acquire the contents of the mind through experience. As the mind acquires new contents, they are assimilated
with the existing contents. This occurs in what Herbart called the
apperceptive mass. Within the mind new apperceptions or presenta-
tions unite with older apperceptions and struggle to rise from the un-
conscious level of mind to the conscious. Herbart is recognized as
one of the leading psychologists of his day. He attempted to make the
rules of psychology as binding and incontrovertible as those of physics.

In the history of American realism we find, as we might expect,
at least two different schools of epistemological thought. While both
schools admit the existence and externality of the "real" world, they
view the problem of how we can know it in different ways.

The New Realists were so-called because they emerged as a reaction to idealism. Where idealism gives special status to mind, seeing
it as basically the stuff from which all other things are created, the
New Realists, particularly the American school, rejected this notion,
giving mind no special status and viewing it as part of nature. This
position was first stated in 1912 by six professors of philosophy. Ralph
Barton Perry, Edwin B. Holt, Walter T. Marvin, Edward G. Spauld-
ing, Walter B. Pitkin, and W. P. Montague published, in 1912, the
statement of this position under the title, *The New Realism.*

The first position, or *presentational* view of knowledge, holds
that we know the real object as it exists. This is the position of the
New Realists. When one perceives something, it is the same thing that
exists in the "real" world. Thus, mind becomes the relationship between the subject and the object. In this school of thought there can
be no major problems of truth, since the correspondence theory is
ideally applicable. This theory states that a thing is true as it corres-
ponds to the real world. Since knowledge is by definition correspondence, it must be true.

Not all realists felt that they could support the position of the New
Realists. Thus, in 1916 another group was formed consisting of Durant Drake, Arthur O. Lovejoy, James B. Pratt, George Santayana, Roy
W. Sellars, Arthur K. Rogers, and C. A. Strong. The major difference
between the New Realists and this new group, the Critical Realists,
seems to have centered on epistemological considerations. The Critical Realists felt that man could not know the world directly but only
through certain vehicles or essences. Thus, objects are not presented

to consciousness but are represented. It was felt by the Critical Realists that this position was the only way to explain errors of perception. In 1920 the Critical Realists published their platform under the title *Essays in Critical Realism.*

The Critical Realists take a different view of knowledge and one which seems better able to account for errors in perception. Their position is a *representational* view. This position holds that although something exists in reality our knowledge is not of it, but of a representation of it. Thus, the Critical Realist is faced with the question of how knowledge, if it is not direct apprehension of something, gets to our mind. Or, to put it in the terms of the Critical Realists, what is the vehicle of knowledge? We do not know the world directly (epistemological monism) but by means of some intervening phenomenon (epistemological dualism) which affects how we perceive and think about the world. The vehicle differs for different supporters of this school. Some hold that it is a mental vehicle and not a part of the physical world, while others suggest that the vehicle is neutral and not an intrinsic part of the physical *or* mental world. Are there some special categories preexistent ("built ins") in the mind? That is, are some ideas innate and part of the mind which determine how we perceive and organize the objects of the material world?

Classic realism remains relatively undiluted from its Platonic and Aristotelian sources in the writings of Harry S. Broudy, who still argues that truth does not need a knower to be true. Like the classic writers, he believes that philosophy is and should be normative; since we know what the purposes of education "really" are and what man "really" is, he argues we should use education to aid in the development of the student's fullest potential. Though closely allied with classic realism, a related group called literary humanists is best exemplified by Mortimer J. Adler and Robert M. Hutchins. Though both thinkers are too seminal to appreciate being "labeled," they do share a conviction that the liberal arts curriculum reflected in "The Great Books of the Western World" is more helpful than any set of modern "vocational" or "socialized" options, since it helps man to develop to his fullest humanity and to realize his essence as man which, to their view, has remained constant for all men in places through the centuries. It follows that what the realist seeks in the educated man is not uniqueness as in-depth specialization; rather it is almost the Renaissance ideal of the well rounded "civilized" man of many interests, vast humanity, and basic decency in harmony with the worlds (?) of science and man. It is their belief that the purpose of education is preservative of the known values of our cultural heritage rather than some rebellious departure from it. In this they feel they are supported by the universality of man's struggle on earth reflected in the great poetry, essays, novels, and tragedies of world literature. They have also attempted to distill what they think is best, most universal, and true in philosophy, science, and mathematics. As is true for other realists as well, Hutchins and Broudy oppose anything less than an absolute standard for morality; they would disagree with the fashionable anthropologists who remind us that it is men in their tribal arrangements who themselves make the "laws" about what is acceptable or unacceptable in any given society.

As the realists as a "school" of thinkers view the value problem (axiology) they are in agreement about the existence of natural laws — though they may disagree among themselves about what they are or what one ought to do in conduct (ethics). What is good? (ethics): As has been pointed out, the realist believes in natural law. Man can know this natural law; and to live the good life, must live by it. All man's experience is rooted in the regularities of the universe or this natural law. In the realm of ethics this natural law is referred to as the moral law. It was to this that Thomas Jefferson had reference when, in the Declaration of Independence, he spoke of man's "unalienable rights" and "the laws of nature." These moral laws have the same existential status as the law of gravity or the economic laws of Adam Smith and they are the object of education.

To the realist, beauty is found in the order of nature. A beautiful art form reflects the logic and order of nature and natural law. Nature in the raw is thought to show evidence of a plan or design. Art must attempt to imitate or reflect the order of nature. The more faithfully an art form does this, the more aesthetically pleasing it is. Thus, a good color photograph of a sunflower would be far more aesthetically pleasing than a Van Gogh painting of the same subject.

From the foregoing, it should now be apparent that the social position of this philosophy would closely approximate that of idealism. Since the concern of this position is with the known, and with the transmission of the known, it tends to conserve the cultural heritage, which it views as all those things that man has learned about natural laws and the order of the universe over untold centuries. The realist position sees society as operating in the framework of natural law. As man understands the natural law, he will understand society. Since the laws cannot be changed, or even amended, society must function in a particular way. All man can do is serve as a spectator of and, where he as an individual fits into the jigsaw puzzle order of natural law, participate in the society. Basically, however, man serves to pass on what is known to be true knowledge of the social laws.

The realist's primary educational aim is to teach those things and values which will lead to the good life. But, for the realist, the good life is equated with one which is in tune with the overarching order of natural law. Thus, the primary aim of education becomes to teach the child the natural and moral law, or at least as much of it as we know, so that his generation may lead the right kind of life, one in tune with the laws of the universe. Clearly, like idealism, the philosophy is mentalistic and rationalistic.

To the realist, the student is a functioning organism which, through his sensory experience, he can perceive the natural order of the world. The pupil, as viewed by many realists, is not totally free, but is subject to certain natural laws. It is not at all uncommon to find realists advocating a behavioristic psychology. The pupil must come to recognize and respond to the coercive order of nature in those cases where he cannot control his experiences, while learning to control his experiences where such control is possible. At its most extreme, the pupil is viewed as a machine which can be programmed in a manner similar to the programming of a computer. In any case, drill and exercise form a primary part of the student's school experience.

The teacher for the realist is simply a guide. The real world exists, and the teacher is responsible for introducing the student to it. To do this, he of course uses lectures, demonstrations, and sensory experience. The teacher does not do this in a random or haphazard way. He must not only introduce the student to nature, but show him the regularities, "the rhythm" of nature so that he may come to understand natural law. Both the teacher and the student are spectators; but while the student looks at the world through innocent eyes, the teacher must explain it to him as well as he is able from his vantage point of increased sophistication. For this reason, the teacher's own biases and personality should be as muted as possible. In order to give the student as much accurate information as quickly and effectively as possible, the realist may advocate the use of teaching machines to remove the teacher's bias from factual presentation. The whole concept of teaching machines is compatible with the idea that man is a machine and can be programmed. Teaching is in this view best when it is most objective, abstract, and dehumanized.

For the realist, subject matter is the matter of the physical universe, the real world, taught in such a way as to show the orderliness underlying the universe. The laws of nature, the realist believes, are most readily understood through the subjects of nature, namely science in all its many branches. As we study nature and gather data, we can see the underlying order of the universe. The highest form of order is found in mathematics. Mathematics is a precise, abstract, symbolic system for describing the laws of the universe. Even in the social sciences we find the realist's conception of the universe shaping the subject matter. The social sciences are viewed as dealing with the mechanical and natural forces which bear on human behavior. The realist views the curriculum as reducible to knowledge that can be measured. For, as E. L. Thorndike put it in his now famous dictum, "whatever exists exists in some amount." It follows that realists are opposed to individualized instruction, pleasurable hours on the playing field or the self-expression of art and music.

The method of the realists involves teaching for the mastery of facts in order to develop an understanding of natural law. This can be done by teaching both the materials and their application. In fact, real knowledge comes only when the organism can organize the data of experience. The realist prefers to use inductive logic, going from the particular facts of sensory experience to the more general laws arising from this data. The general laws are seen as universal natural law. In his method, the realist depends on motivating the student. But this is not difficult, since many realists view the interests of the learner as fundamental urges toward an understanding of natural law rooted in our common sense. The understanding of natural law comes through the organizing of data through insight. The realist in his method approves anything which involves learning through sensory experience, whether it be direct or indirect. Not only are field trips considered valuable, but the realist advocates the use of films, filmstrips, records, television, radio, and any other audiovisual aids which might serve in the place of direct sensory experience. This does not mean that the realist denies the validity of symbolic knowledge. Rather, it implies that the symbol has no special existential status, but is viewed simply as a means of communicating about, or representing, the real world.

Few moderns are either consistent idealists or realists; more probably, they automatically shift from one position to the other, depending on the subject under investigation. This blend of the two philosophies is called Essentialism and arose historically as a consequence of the unsolved dilemma of the epistemological problems of realism in relation to idealism. For example, to many moderns it would seem impossible for a man to say he was a Christian scientist. Is he both? At the same time? Is he being Christian when he functions as a scientist? Is he being scientific when he functions as a Christian? Should his acts be consistent? The same impudent questions could be asked of one who fancied himself a Lutheran philosopher. Certainly men put on different heads for different jobs less self-consciously than they change vacuum cleaner attachments. The essentialist often combines two of most noble and well intentioned philosophies and becomes a kind of fundamentalist about the educative process, illustrating the worst of both.

Essentialism is not an independent philosophical position, but rather an educational position which is an amalgam of idealism and realism. Its roots lie in the similarities to be found in the epistemological and social views of the two positions. The essentialists believe that truth exists and can be known. Whether this truth is of the nature of mind, as the idealists have it, or of the nature of matter, as the realists prefer, is of little significance. Education's responsibility is to teach the known. That which is known of the real world is taught through the sciences and mathematics, while that which is concerned with the ideal nature of man and the universe is learned through the humanities. It is not the school's responsibility to worry about the future when so much of the past must be known. One cannot, says the essentialist, concern himself in school with the future. The school's responsibility is to conserve the cultural heritage; and to do this, only the known facts can be taught. When this is done, the future will have been adequately prepared for. The world is best viewed as governed and determined; and before we can explore the future, we must be familiar with the order of the world as it really exists.

This issue of determining and assessing what is most real and valuable still largely determines curriculum content from nursery school to graduate school. By some assessment, the real core of the curriculum is thought to be sacred. Our Jimmy or Judy is taught forms of higher mathematics in high school in an age of adding machines and computers. Our child is taught penmanship in the age of the office machine and typewriters. He is taught our Saber-Toothed curriculum of fish catching with his bare hands even though we have moved inland to become ranchers where the lakes are so polluted that the poisoned fish have all long since sunk to the bottom. The parent is told that there is really nothing wrong with mathematics which is "really" good for Jimmy who wants badly to become a cook, but there must be something wrong with Jimmy. If we disagree, we are as likely to be referred to counselors to be "adjusted" as our Jimmy or Judy. Yet parents themselves often resist any tampering with the basic curriculum. Reading, writing, and arithmetic are defended against the plea to make room in the curriculum for courses in The Dope Culture, Sex Education, or Abnormal Psychology. Evidently, we don't mind students being taught the rudiments of physical sciences; but we refuse to consider social problems as being of a similar order. The "real" sciences cannot, so the argument goes, "really" help us with these kinds of problems which we fancy have to be explained by some totally different set of criteria—like "moral decay" or "permissiveness."

Essentialism is not a philosophy; it is an admission that one cannot "get it all together" or "get straight." It is not conducive to problem solving, but it is sleep producing. Were the position consciously adopted, one could speak better of it: The universe is more manageable if we can isolate it into different compartments, but it is not philosophy to always assign the left-hand tasks in isolation from the right. Neither can our notions about moral and/or physical law operate in isolation from practice or practice operate distinct from them. To act as the "Romans do in Rome" on Monday and as "A Cretan in Crete" on Tuesday on the Grand Tour is as unfortunate and comic as it is schizoid. A philosophy which does consciously and consistently manage to juggle the world of spirit and the world of substance is perennialism, which provides a poetic picture of what is Caesar's and what is God's. Perennialism does synthesize the idealistic and realistic positions to its own satisfaction.

SUGGESTED READINGS

BECK, ROBERT N. *Perspectives in Philosophy.* New York: Holt, Rinehart & Winston, 1961. Though the book is designed as a text, it can be read by non-students of academic philosophy. Though all of the major sections are first-rate, the chapter on classic realism is outstanding, for it contains current realists as well as the great thinkers of the past.

DRAKE, DURANT, et al. (eds.). *Essays in Critical Realism: A Cooperative Study of the Problems of Knowledge.* New York: Peter Smith, 1941. This book provides a cross-section of essays sympathetic to idealism by outstanding thinkers.

DUPUIS, ADRIAN M., and ROBERT NORDBERG. *Philosophy and Education.* Milwaukee, Wisc.: Bruce Publishing Company, 1964. This book has the great value of making and keeping the distinctions between idealism, realism, and perennialism clear. It is comprehensible to laymen.

DURANT, WILL. *The Story of Philosophy.* New York: The Pocket Library, 1926. This famous book, readily available in paperback, has an outstanding chapter on Aristotle, the first great realist.

HOLT, EDWIN B., et al. *The New Realism: Cooperative Studies in Philosophy.* New York: Macmillan, 1912. Here is not only a review of the history of realism as a philosophical position, but also the new realists.

WYNNE, JOHN P. *Theories of Education.* New York: Harper & Row, 1963. In addition to the standard divisions into thematic frames of reference, the book contains keen insights into the relationships between psychological and philosophical theories.

CHAPTER 3

Perennialism

As a philosophy of education, perennialism is often divided into a lay and an ecclesiastical branch, but this division has disadvantages, since it is Robert M. Hutchins and Mortimer Adler who are usually classed as the lay perennialists; and we have already shown their affinities to idealism and why they are best classed under the rubric of realism. But Robert Maynard Hutchins, Mortimer Adler, and Stringfellow Barr have supported the idea of a university-level curriculum based on a selection of "Great Books" which have withstood the test of time and are therefore "truer" than the non-classics which have only a short-range appeal. Among the titles are many from the pre-Christian era and many freethinkers who do not espouse adherence to any specific dogma. What they do adhere to is the position that there are everlasting, and even pre-existing values to which we must return; in this sense they are perennialists.

As we discuss the ecclesiastical branch of perennialism, we shall not confine ourselves only to the Roman Catholic church and its neo-Thomism or neo-scholasticism. Besides, when churchmen are speaking of educational philosophy, they speak of perennialism to avoid undue confusion. Obviously, since there are many forms of persuasion, one could be, for example, a Lutheran or Jewish perennialist. What they share is a metaphysical frame of reference, a strict ontology — hierarchy of values — and a supernatural basis for distinguishing between the things of the sacred and secular worlds as well as a rationale for non-public schools.

Each has a view of man and a program of action for developing students to act toward their fellow men in conformity with prescribed beliefs and a related code of conduct. In each case, ethics are prescribed, and the school is entrusted with the teaching of morality.

In its best known and most consistently and frequently used form, perennialism is a developed form of realism advocated first by St. Thomas Aquinas and based upon Aristotelian realism. It was Aristotle who contributed most to the basic realist position with his conceptions of form and matter. Form was viewed as being at the apex of the pyramid or hierarchy, whereas matter was at the base. Matter existed as pure potentiality; it acquired meaning only as form—some principle of organization—was imposed upon it. It was form that was seen as the principle of actuality. All things were composed of form and matter. Man, for example, had a physical being composed of matter and a mind which was composed of form. Form was equated with pure rationality, while matter was composed of pure materiality.

For the first thousand years of Christianity, the works of Aristotle were lost. Further, the Christians had no use for such works of "The Pagan" as were preserved in the Near East and among the Eastern orthodox. The Christian theologians were concerned with presenting the message of their faith to the people as simply as possible. For Christian philosophers this long period was not a time to be concerned with any aspects of philosophy other than the elaboration and justification of the dogmas (those "truths" accepted without the support of demonstration or experience) taught in Scripture and through the church. To such churchmen as St. Augustine in the fifth century, man was a spiritual creature and the world was full of God's love for man. Education in this view is intended to enable the student to realize his spiritual potential and rise above selfishness, pettiness, and greed.

In the thirteenth century, Saint Thomas Aquinas, "The Angelic Doctor," used the work of Aristotle being reintroduced to Europe from the far more scientifically advanced Near East and, after accepting his form-and-matter thesis, added to it the concept of existence. He superimposed upon Aristotelianism the God and world view of the Roman Catholic church. Less charitably, we could say he offset the threat of Aristotle's primitive scientific position to the established dogmas and articles of faith of medieval Catholicism by Christianizing Aristotle and thus provided a rationale for such basic church doctrines as the Trinity and the virgin birth. By an act of thrilling audacity, he incorporated the work of Aristotle into the Christian framework and "completed" Aristotle's system. Some say he preserved both scientific attitudes and faith in the process and paved the road to the Renaissance; others say he delayed the Renaissance by ushering in an age of vicious theological argument. St. Thomas reconciled the Christian principles of his faith with the realism of Aristotle, by insisting that beyond essence (the combination of form and matter), lay Existence. Aristotle, according to Aquinas, was right in what he said, but failed to raise the question of the existence of essences. Thus, for

Aquinas, essence becomes the principle of potentiality while Existence becomes the principle of actuality. Pure Existence (or Pure Actuality) is, of course, God. We can know Pure Existence only through revelation, although we can know *about* it through reason. In this manner Aquinas postulated a realistic world in which man must make his way while preparing for life in the hereafter. While reason is able to deal with the world of nature, revelation deals with the world beyond nature. Finally for Aquinas, faith must always take over when reason has reached its limits.

It must be recalled that the medieval churchmen were not in their view being reactionary. The rudiments of the methods of science and its boundaries were scarcely understood by them. Besides, they believed in belief; that is, they had faith in faith and did not doubt the dogmas upon which their religious views were founded. In fact, they could argue quite convincingly that, since everyone knew of the truth of the Trinity, the correct interpretation of the Scriptures, and the nature and destiny of man as foretold in the Bible and the writings of the fathers of the church, they were indeed being scientific. Their actions followed from their beliefs. They could demonstrate with remarkable ingenuity, logical consistency, and textual reference "demonstrations" of the truth of their view. These elaborate proofs were further supplemented by the mystic visions of the saints, miracles, and the authority of the church. It is therefore fair to echo the standard claim against medievalism that it made philosophy a handmaiden to religion. Indeed, one could even say it made philosophy secondary to theology with all its faith in things not seen. After all, thinkers would say, we do not understand in order to believe; we believe in order to understand. No secular view of politics or government was for the medieval church scholar ever self-justifying, regardless of the consequences; secular states must also be judged by a higher morality than a materialistic view of the world could applaud.

The perennialists, then, cannot or will not view the universe apart from an ontological hierarchy of values based upon a supernatural metaphysics apart from all man-made logics and sciences. What they may not acknowledge is that their view is equally man-made and that their fond hopes and unflagging feelings of certainty are not proofs of anything except their zeal and the intensity of their beliefs. To claim that the heart has its reasons which the head cannot understand or that the test of a belief is its impossibility is not a proof; it is merely a counterclaim too often based on a rejection of scientific evidence. It should not surprise us that such a view is reactionary and that on vital issues it prizes orthodoxy and established authority above inquiry and originality. For a controversial example from the contemporary world, we could cite all the probable consequences of overpopulation and contrast them with the official church and papal view. It is hard for a non-Christian to believe that "God will provide" for the billions predicted to inhabit the earth with its diminishing natural resources or that earthquakes which kill thousands could be part of a divine plan which shows the glory of God and the insignificance of man and his view of himself. If every typhoon and volcanic eruption is planned by God for some good reason, little is left for man but to endure as passively as possible. Such a view does not encourage planning by man to tamper with God's will by building dams, sponsoring medical research, or helping the victims of natural disasters whose beliefs are different from our own.

In summary, the perennialist believes that all things are composed of form and matter which make up their essence. But in order for things to be in the world, they must have Existence. Essence is the principle of potentiality, while Existence is the principle of actuality. For the perennialist, Existence is of a higher order than essence. It stands in the same relationship to essence that form stood to matter in the Aristotelian ontology. At the top of the hierarchy is Pure Existence, or Being. The essence of Being is Existence. For the ecclesiastical perennialist this Being is equated with God. God cannot be known except through faith and revelation (although we may have knowledge of God's existence through purely rational means). He is Pure Actuality. Thus, the ontology of the perennialists is a two-sided coin. On the one side is the natural world, open to reason, while on the other is the supernatural realm, open only through revelation, faith, and intuition. Truths are revealed to man by God through some external source or omen such as a burning bush or miracle which seems impossible of scientific explanation and defies the laws of cause and effect which operate in the natural world. Intuition is a direct and emotional mystic experience of some new, immediate, and self-evident knowledge of the "truth" about the reality of self, others, data, or the nature of God. Such intense, blinding visions accompanied by feelings of certitude and well being are testified to in the writings of saints and visionary poets like Blake and Dickinson.

Science deals with the first side of the coin, but the spiritual side of the coin is beyond its reach. The perennialist ontology is teleological, holding that man and the universe are moving toward a prescribed end. This end is realization of the principle of actuality, or Absolute Being. The perennialist teleology can be known through faith, dogma, intuition, and revelation. The lay perennialist would find all the foregoing acceptable. He would not reject the Aristotelian concept of reality. He would agree that the universe has a logic, and he would even accept the concept of Pure Being, *as long as it was not given a special religious status or theological stature*. The lay perennialist sees no need for equating Being with God and thus making it something to be feared and worshiped. Further, he would be less likely to consciously accept such a dualistic view of the world or to give over his universal definition of the nature of man to some exclusive religious group. To him, questions are as important as answers.

As we should expect, the perennialist has a view of knowledge and truth (epistemology) radically different from the modern philosophies of education. The perennialist believes that to know the truth about something is to know its essence. As has been indicated in the foregoing, to know the entire truth about reality we must rely on intuition, faith, or revelation. Since the perennialist ontology is teleological, the hard core of reality is logical, permanent, and unchanging. Truth, therefore, is also logical, permanent, and unchanging. Man tends toward knowledge. His mind is basically curious; thus, he needs little special prodding to start him on his epistemological expedition. The perennialist believes that there are certain things that are self-evident and that the structure of knowledge rests upon those self-evident truths that we know. A self-evident truth is always an analytic statement or one that contains, in its subject, its predicate. For example, God is good. This type of statement is opposed to synthetic statements which depend upon our experience, such as excessive martini drinking causes drunkenness. Analytic statements are logically true. Such statements, however, as the empiricists point out, although necessarily true by definition or convention, do not yield knowledge of the experiential universe. This is not to imply that they cannot have meaning, it is simply to indicate that they cannot give us new knowledge.

Perennialists see the analytic statement as a self-evident truth that may be known apart from all empirical experience. It is, for them, a first principle. Man can intuit first principles, such as there is an afterlife. These self-evident truths open, for the perennialist, a whole realm of truth that cannot be reached by science. For the lay perennialist truth can be known through reason and intuition. For the ecclesiastical perennialist there is, added to these two ways of knowing, the certitude of revelation which is given to man. While intuiting is an activity of man, man is simply the recipient of revelation given from a source external to man.

Both the lay and the ecclesiastical perennialists rely heavily on reason. This takes the form of Aristotelian logic, and is basically deductive. Induction, however, is not rejected, since the perennialists, as realists, start with the experiences of the senses and must organize these into general rules. Two warnings about the perennialist epistemology must be pointed out. First, first principles should not be confused with clever sayings, with slogans, or with proverbs. While such statements as "a fool and his money are soon parted," may be commonly true, first principles are always and universally true. Second, there is little justification for the argument that the perennialist's view of reason was only a way to support belief. Revelation is simply an independent way of arriving at the correct conclusion. The discoveries of geology and biology and archeology do not, in their view, disprove divine creation; they are simply alternate theories which are unable to tell the whole truth. The ecclesiastical perennialist would argue that faith is not proof of reason, nor is reason proof of faith. They are simply two routes to the same truth, either of which can serve to verify the other. However, the test of one's faith is still too often taken to be the rejection of scientific evidence; it is still possible for some to believe a proposition because it is impossible to consider from a scientific frame of reference.

In axiology, the perennialists view values and what is good and right in conduct, ethics, as we might expect. Just as man tends toward knowledge, so he tends toward the moral life. And just as knowledge is attained through reason, so the moral life is the life consonant with reason. The good act is the act controlled by man's rationality. But man does not always act in terms of his rationality, he is sometimes controlled by his will, which may err, or his desires. The good man is one whose will is habituated to, and subservient to, the intellect. The ecclesiastical perennialists hold that where sin exists (the will acting in opposition to intellect), forgiveness may be attained if the sinner can show his intentions were good. By the same token, if a man does not know he is wrong, he cannot be held responsible for his acts. For the perennialist, there is a values hierarchy and there are certain ultimate values that are not dependent on man. These values may be found through reason. In the hierarchy of values, the ecclesiastical perennialist places the greatest importance on man's duty to God and the school is the place where such duties are taught.

As a part of the wonderful consistency of so vast and comprehensive a system of educational philosophy, the perennialist does not view the contemplation of what is beautiful, aesthetic, apart from what is good and right in conduct, ethics. Like the Platonic idealists, whom they so much resemble, and many of the famous nineteenth-century Romantic poets in rebellion against the sordidness of modern urban industrial life, they believe "Beauty is truth, truth beauty,—that is all/Ye know on earth, and all ye need to know." Just as man tends toward knowledge and morality, he tends toward beauty. We know something is beautiful when we respond to it immediately and with pleasure. Man tends to be creative, he desires to give to his material the meaning that is potential in it. Art, therefore, is immediately self-evident. The artist intuits meaning rather than approaching it logically, although he may appreciate a work of art through the pleasure it gives the intellect and because it pleases the supernatural God who designed a beautiful world. The most beautiful work of art is that which celebrates the divine order and symbolizes some spiritual truth. Art is, in this sense, propaganda.

Consequently, there are two aims involved in the perennialist educational philosophy. The ecclesiastical perennialists see the school as concerned with the secular in education and particularly the training of the intellect, but in addition to this they see a second aim carefully interwoven with this. They view education as a moral and religious undertaking. The ecclesiastical perennialists believe that the school cannot separate itself from the study of those things that have come to man through faith and revelation, and it is for this reason that the Catholic church in America has continued to maintain a separate school system in order to permeate its teachings with its moral and religious convictions. Freedom of religion guarantees the continued existence of both public and parochial schools. Catholics, Quakers, Seventh Day Adventists, Jews, and others are guaranteed this right by the constitution as it has been interpreted by Supreme Court decisions and legislation.

Intrinsic for the perennialist, subject matter falls into two areas. The lay perennialists emphasize the subject matter of the intellect, while the ecclesiastical perennialists include the subject matter of the spirit. Obviously at the elementary school level the emphasis is on basic skills—reading, writing, and arithmetic—as well as the subject matter of reason and the intellect. The latter is any subject matter which has a high degree of structure, such as languages. Not only does language develop the ability to reason, it requires memorization and will power. There is a tendency to reject the humanities per se as well as the social sciences and to emphasize science, mathematics, literature, geography, and history. In the later school years the emphasis shifts to grammar, rhetoric, and logic, as well as mathematics. In the ecclesiastical wing, where the search is for God rather than for

Pure Being, there is an appropriate concern for the subject matter of True Religion. This, for example, means that for devout Roman Catholics there is *The Index*, a list of books that may not be read, since they blaspheme and are in error about the True Faith. Included in the curriculum is a good deal of material on church dogma, faith, and revelation as well as ceremonies and prayers.

The method of teaching for the perennialist is rooted in mental discipline and the training of the intellect through the discipline inherent in the subject matter. Since the child has a natural tendency to learn, the basis of the perennialist method is cooperation with the natural tendency of the student toward reason. The perennialist methodology relies heavily upon the use of lectures to enlighten the student while he follows his natural curiosity under the moral authority of the teacher. Other techniques considered important by the perennialists are memorization of materials, and for the ecclesiastical perennialists, recitation of the catechism. It is important to them for the student to know the answers to profound questions he will meet later on in life. His training prepares him so he will know what to do when he is confronted with new and challenging situations. In the perennialists' view, the secular public schools are not nearly so comprehensive and are not equipped to instruct the young in morality, ethics, or conduct.

The teacher, to the perennialist, is a mental disciplinarian of highly developed logical skills, capable of teaching correct logical thinking and employing reason with his students. The teacher must have the ability to work with the natural tendencies of the students toward reason. He must serve as a benevolent taskmaster, exercising the minds of the students in order to help them develop their rational faculties. For the ecclesiastical perennialist, there is also the role of spiritual leader to be filled. This involves the teaching of those dogmas which must be accepted on faith alone, as well as the dogmas and revelations which verify the positions arrived at logically. Thus, besides having been trained in logic, the teacher must have the proper spiritual orientation. This is not all, however. Since the teacher is to train the students in reason, memory, and will power, he must certainly have these three qualities if he is to help the student on the road to developing these faculties.

The student is seen as a rational being with tendencies toward truth and knowledge. But the learner also has a spiritual side. It is the responsibility of the school to help him develop both capacities. The rational powers of the learner tend to be viewed from a position of faculty psychology. In this view, the mind is thought to have different potentials, all of which must be carefully developed. Thus, the faculty of reason is trained through the formal discipline of those subjects with the most logical organization. The faculty of memory is trained by having students memorize, and the faculty of will is trained by having the students engage in tasks which are unpleasant enough to require a high degree of perseverance to complete. Between these three types of exercise the student develops to the fullest his basic faculties: reason, memory, and will. Ideally, the perennialist would tend toward developing a standardized, typical kind of student-citizen as the product of the careful, guided curriculum.

The perennialists have what may be viewed as a regressive social philosophy. They would have us solve our twentieth-century problems by turning back the clock to a system of beliefs prevalent in the thirteenth century. They would have us turn the clock back to a time when the source of authority was external to man and when, they would have us believe, man was at a moral and spiritual peak, from which he has declined. The moral, intellectual, and spiritual revolution that the perennialists advocate is seen as coming, of necessity, from church and university. The lower schools will have little to do with social change, since the school must transcend society and deal with the teaching of first principles, the permanent bases of Eternal Truth.

SUGGESTED READINGS

BUTLER, DONALD J. *Four Philosophies and Their Practice in Education and Religion,* rev. ed. New York: Harper Brothers, 1957. Butler is primarily concerned with neo-scholasticism as a form of realism. His emphasis is on the ecclesiastical perennialists and the role of God in the philosophy.

DRAKE, WILLIAM E. *Intellectual Foundations of Modern Education.* Columbus, Ohio: Charles E. Merrill, 1967. This book argues for a broad-based religious humanism as against all current secular educational philosophy, including pragmaticism, analysis, and existentialism.

ENCYCLICAL LETTER. *Divini Magistic of His Holiness Pope Pius XI.* New York: The American Press, 1936. Here is an unusually clear restatement of the duty of the Catholic church to maintain its educational objectives often at variance with the worldly thinking of any specific age.

GOSEN, SISTER MARY DE SALES, C.P.P.S. *The Status of Education as a Science.* New York: Pageant Press, 1963. Here is a lucid statement for rejecting secular definitions of science in favor of the all-inclusive science of theology as a solid base for organizing educational experiences in parochial schools.

JAHSMANN, ALLAN HART. *What's Lutheran in Education?* St. Louis: Concordia Publishing Company, 1960. Here we have a statement of the perennialist rationale for directing the activities of the schools within the Missouri Synod. It shows how inquiry is guided by Lutheran theology.

MORRIS, VAN CLEVE. *Philosophy and the American School.* Boston: Houghton Mifflin, 1961. This amazingly comprehensive book deals with perennialism under the heading of neo-Thomism. This text is of great value in considering all the educational philosophies in relation to one another.

WARD, LEO R. *Philosophy of Education.* Chicago: Henry Regnery, 1963. The book provides a frame of reference far broader than most modern educators would admit for viewing questions of value, meanings, aims, and objectives of education.

CHAPTER 4

Pragmatism

Pragmatism is widely misunderstood by those both in and out of the profession of education. When the layman speaks of pragmatism, he is talking about what William James called the "cash value of ideas." In this view ideas are simply tools to be used in the solution of practical problems; this misunderstanding confirms the American prejudice against speculative thought in favor of being "up and doing." The notion is that all speculation which does not immediately result in profits is silly. From this, the crude assumption is often suggested that the ends justify the means: If a country won't negotiate, for example, bomb the hell out of it until it does. It is understood as meaning that ideas help us get what we want rather than understanding what we get. This misconception fosters the mistaken notion that ends and means are not interwoven in a complex fabric or that theory does not have to interact with experience if any philosophy is to have the value of self-survival and be a trustworthy guide to the organization of experience. This is counter to the very nature of pragmatism, which professes to be a reasonable and sane philosophy which reminds us of the essential interdependence of theory with the elaborate, difficult choices to be made in a world of terrifying complexity and dizzyingly accelerated rates of change.

For another example of the popular misuse of the term, we have only to consider that at some time each of us has been encouraged to be pragmatic. What this seems to mean is that one should sacrifice his principles in acknowledgment of the vicious powers of the world in order that he can eventually get what he wants by "playing the game" or agreeing with a complacent majority. This disregard of what he may perceive to be his case or what he might call justice in order to achieve private, selfish ends by not presenting the evidence which supports his point of view is also applauded as pragmatic. It is "the company way" of the hollow organization man and the teacher who does not press for needed curricular reform for fear of losing his job.

46

The true pragmatists cringe when a Willy Brandt or a Nixon is described by the popular press as "pragmatic." The pragmatist disdains what he regards as cowardly halfway measures which are merely "adjustive" to popular sentiment or the current political realities. What the consistent pragmatists strive for instead is to get to the roots of a problem and solve it by some genuine "adaptation" which will stand against the ravages of time. In this sense, some are, ironically, very "idealistic" and impatient of compromise. To critics of pragmatism, this reluctance to understand why viable nations make haste slowly only after myriad, accumulated compromises is a mark against it; the critics remind us that the tortuous road to European economic, cultural, and governmental unity cannot be attained by superimposed plans or impatience.

Pragmatism ideally aims at intellectually honest solutions based upon an objective and dispassionate scientific analysis of all the evidence before any solution is even considered. This is genuine reflective problem solving. It aims scrupulously for honesty and the right —not necessarily the easiest—solution to the problem under investigation, based solely upon the quality of the evidence as defined by science. Action must not precede thought nor action be taken without a carefully developed plan which reaches the desired consequences. In this regard, the solution is right only if it is public in the sense that reasonable men employing the same careful checks on their investigation come to the same conclusion from a careful analysis of the same evidence relating to the same problem. This indeed makes great demands on individual men. Pragmatists are fond of saying that a solution which is a solution for only one person or a specific group of persons with similar selfish interests is not a solution. Indeed, to encourage such sets of different answers makes of the world a place of chaos and warring factions rather than a place where what they call the method of intelligence prevails and makes possible rational planning for the good of all.

Pragmatism, then, is not a short-range, makeshift philosophy which can be immediately applied to each situation in isolation from the elaborate context of the difficulty with its myriad related problems. In theory, pragmatism considers all the contingencies and prepares for them; in scientific parlance, we would say it can control the variables. For a crude example, the pragmatists in theory would not apply a mend-on patch to a rotten pair of work pants. Indeed, pragmatism makes much of philosophy as vision and often sets goals incapable of immediate realization because men still insist upon being Muslims or Jews, Catholics or Protestants, Buddhists or Hindus first and pragmatists second, if at all. This explains in part why pragmatism is not a popular American export to developing countries and often does not work for them in application.

The differences inherent in multi-cultural diversified societies might not be solved if all men suddenly became pragmatists. Indeed, the result might be even more talk and even less action. The Western definition of progress, to them, is an unrealistic impertinence. Yet these problems must be carefully thought out or their attempts at reform are unguided and uncoordinated "hit and miss" and "trial and error." Pragmatism attempts to provide calm and dispassionate analysis in the place of panic or repression in the name of order, yet we must admit that the peoples of countries chasing the rainbow of rising expectations have not been prepared by their formal schooling to be realistic problem solvers. Indeed, critical thinking and the habit of intellectual discontent with the status quo fostered by pragmatism can contribute to the breakdown of established social orders and add to widespread frustration. It can also be argued that for all our talk of the value of problem solving, our schools have not prepared us to function as genuinely pragmatic adults. It is therefore essential that we understand the evolution of pragmatism and what being pragmatic requires of us so we can accept or reject it.

As a formal philosophy, pragmatism is a relatively recent development in American thought. Though the term is new, the roots of pragmatism may be found throughout Western history. In its radical suspicions of past speculative and rationalistic philosophical systems, it is brusquely American. It contains elements of the Enlightenment in its refusal to believe that the future must duplicate the past. Like the Enlightenment, it is opposed to all uncritically accepted authority, tradition, custom, intuition, or raw common-sense attitudes. Like the Enlightenment, it tends to be optimistic about the future and man's ability to control and order his destiny by the proper employment of science. Unlike the Enlightenment, it does not deduce what our behavior should be from sets of metaphysical statements about the structure of the universe or the essense or nature of man. What man is to the pragmatists' view is dependent upon his hereditary and specific environment; we can, they argue, change man's habits of action by enlightened programs of enriched or changed environments. Indeed, pragmatism argues that all such speculations about the constant nature of all men are folly and not sanctioned by science, which is open ended—fluid and dynamic.

At best, the human mind is a tool to be used instrumentally in the resolution of problems, personal and social, and not some special faculty which achieves its fullest realization in the contemplation of given philosophical questions. In other words, they reject the faulty psychology of the traditional views of educational philosophy. Such questions as the nature of man, they persist, endure not because of their importance, but because of their silliness. Traditional philosophers cannot, they maintain, prove their assumptions, which are extra-logical; and they are incapable of providing a basis for consent without the guesswork of showing how their assumptions relate to the brute world of experience by questionable deductive logic. The most startling form of this argument which traditionalists would regard as shocking anti-intellectualism is expressed by Sidney Hook, who discounts all traditional philosophies as "garrulous nonsense," since they are based upon some untestable predefined religions or metaphysical, axiological, or epistemological precepts which determine in advance what all our conclusions will be.

As Hook states his interpretation of educational philosophy in his essay "The Scope of Philosophy," metaphysics, axiology, and epistemology are at best only tenuously and imaginatively related to educational theory and practice. Even, he argues, if men agree in theory or share membership in any philosophical school of educational thought, they will not automatically agree about curriculum or teaching methods. Further, those who do agree about curricular objectives and teaching techniques may never share the same philosophical perspective. Consequently, most talk of educational philosophers is futile and evasive. Hook, thus, rejects all absolutes, however founded, from which specific courses of action can be deduced. Instead, to Hook, we examine the alternative possibilities each situation affords before we decide on which of the various alternative courses of action we should implement. This view of pragmatism makes a shambles of the rationale for the careful study of most educational philosophy as usually defined, past and present. We are left not with legislative systems of thought which afford us broad perspectives for viewing our specific educational problems, but with a method for solving particular problems. In Hook's view, even the distinguished professor-editor of the Philosophy of Education Series and author of *Pragmatism in Education,* Ernest Bayles (New York: Harper and Row, 1966) is guilty of trying to show what pragmatism means or implies for educational theory and practice.

It is clear that Hook and the many pragmatists who agree with him have a radically different view of what philosophy is from others. Hook reduces philosophy to method and consigns all talk of the implications of any philosophical school or its "world view" or its meaning and value to the rubbish bin of speculative non-logic. Consequently, most of the study and talk of educational philosophy and the reasons usually given for its study are vain windbaggery. To many, the extreme of Hook's position sounds the death knell of philosophy as we know it. This rejection of all absolutes except the method he chooses makes philosophy a process of relating what we can describe about how men really operate to the shifting material and social environments to which they must relate. At best, in this view, all propositions, no matter how hallowed by time and usage or how much popular support they may have, are merely hypotheses to be tested in action. What we call knowledge at any given time is always subject to change and should be considered no more than a tentative generalization which more and better scientific evidence of the same sort can dethrone.

Though there may have been some social reason in the past for some tribes remaining as nomads to follow their grazing herds, for large families to occur in a time of epidemic and infant mortality, for binding the feet of girls so they could be even more delicate, homebound creatures, for enforcing dietary laws as a means of preserving health, and the practice of widows throwing themselves upon the funeral pyres of their husbands, since such societies made no provisions for the economic self-sufficiency of dependents, the usages of the past are not hallowed and are no sanction for what we should do in a changed world. As the world continues to change at shockingly accelerated rates, how we "do" philosophy and, indeed, even how we define what philosophical problems are, must also be subject to reassessment. By this view, urbanization and technology, for example, give us the problems and conflicts which deserve careful analysis and intelligent planning. Certainly, this view is tough-minded and oriented to the practical solution of what we hope are manageable problems rather than a tender-minded dream of how the universe is constructed, the nature of man, or the contemplation of mythical absolutes. Certainly, this brings us to the cornerstone and primary assumption of this liberal and liberating philosophy — the method of science.

To the true pragmatist, then, what is shared by investigation into educational problems is not anything as vain and abstract as schools of thought or shared philosophical positions. What is shared by those who are alone capable of solving the complex problems related to education is a defensible and workable intellectual method shared by the sciences. To critics, who usually amuse rather than annoy pragmatists, this severe delimitation of the scope and use of all traditional philosophy is as absolute as any school of thought it rejects and has itself apparent implications for both educational theory and practice. Before any further evaluation is made, it might be wise to review American pragmatism as it relates to the model and method of science as the sole criterion for solving educational problems.

Even though there are elements of pragmatic thinking in the life and work of Benjamin Franklin and Ralph Waldo Emerson, who heralded the values of frontier "Self Reliance," it is the brilliant and eccentric Charles Sanders Peirce who deserves the title of founder of pragmatism, Peirce was a natural scientist of keen and broad observation. It seemed to him that traditional philosophy got nowhere; it forever asked the same impossible questions and came up with a variety of impossible and indefensible answers. Philosophers solved no real problems, in his view; they just found more questions equally confusing. To Peirce, this contrasted dramatically with the efficient and measurable results of scientific investigation. Science, then, must deal with the "real" problems and have refined a mode of investigation which yields uniform results which can be weighed and measured quantitatively. Science, then, yields testable results which can be verified, unlike philosophy, which yields only untestable propositions about the unmeasurable qualitative ranking of our own choices.

It follows for Peirce that the *a priori* assumptions we make independently of experience and impossible of scientific verification are all vanity and a weariness of the flesh. Such evaluations of human behavior based on preexistent norms which prescribe what men should do are fictions at best. This is an emphatic denial by Peirce of defending moral choices by any deontological criterion which is subject to debate or makes value judgments or generalizations separate from the consequences they yield, regardless of intention or conviction. Instead, Peirce makes the measure of any proposition the measurable, impersonal consequences subject to investigation by all. It is the ends which are achieved which alone have value; such a view is "teleological" and a rejection of any notion of supreme or intrinsic good. As a favorite example, we could determine whether or not a questionable stone were a diamond by asking it to perform specific operations, like cutting glass. Those who doubted what they were told or had observed could repeat the same process under the same conditions and would be compelled by the evidence to the same conclusion. To Peirce, this was the glory of science: unlike in philosophy, there was no possibility of reaching a conclusion based upon authority, tradition, common sense, or intuition as alternatives to the proof of an experimental investigation of the materials at hand.

Though he could never hold a permanent academic appointment either at Harvard or Johns Hopkins where he taught, because of what was then considered the oddity of his views and his disdain for the moralizing academics of his era, he was the most influential technical philosopher of science America had yet produced. Peirce spent most of his adult life as a careful scientist for the U.S. Geodetic Survey. What work he could get published was printed infrequently in unlikely sources like *Popular Science Monthly*.

Further, Peirce was primarily interested in the ways concepts could be made intelligible or proven to be "poetry." He persisted throughout his long and tragic life to establish a theoretical base for what we would now call pure science. He was interested in the amoral truth, not what men make of it. He feared that moralizing and the impatience that compel men to harness the latest discoveries of science to their fancied needs was contrary to the spirit of science. As a guardian of the logical procedures and rigors of scientific investigation, he castigated the silliness of arguing about whether transubstantiation or consubstantiation were true. Such terms, dependent for their meaning upon symbolism, assigned meaning, dogma of any kind, or private associations — what we would call connotation — have no meaning for science. Consequently, it is only with those aspects of the wine and wafers that can be demonstratively verified, precisely defined by scientific analysis, which have meaning. All competent observers who accept the scientific process by which we arrived at the predicted result (it was wine and wafers) must concur regardless of prior belief or assumption. The fact that the conclusion was neutral, impartial to the needs of the observers, and verified by all is "proof" that science is objective, systematic, and reliable. In other words, intellectual conceptions, hypotheses, which yield predicted practical consequences are true; so concepts can be no greater than the sum total of the verifiable consequences. One wonders if Peirce's ability to settle such disputes by the methods of science could have averted the Crusades or the "Holy" Wars of Europe.

As we see, Peirce was a remarkably consistent spokesman for the scientific attitude. Little of his work was published in his lifetime, and it was not until the 1930s that his collected papers were published and he began to get the scholarly attention his works deserved. Too many, he is still the most overwhelming thinker America has yet produced. It must be cautioned that Peirce was not preoccupied with the emerging social sciences or education except indirectly. Of course, his theories have profound and exciting implications for both. His influence on William James as well as the influence of the utilitarian thinker, Chauncey Wright, was due to their shared memberships in the Metaphysical Club, an informal organization. Peirce's influence on Dewey was less direct, although Peirce was lecturing in logic at the Johns Hopkins University while Dewey was there working on his Ph.D. Most of the influence of Peirce came to Dewey through William James.

It has been said, with some degree of justification, that Henry James wrote like a philosopher, while his brother, William James, wrote like a novelist. Perhaps this explains in part the enduring popularity of both. James sought to popularize and develop the germinal ideas of Peirce, who drubbed him for departing from scientific logic, scientific verifiability as defined by the method of science, and close analysis in favor of speculative system building.

Though James tries hard to be as "tough minded" (his own term) as Peirce and claims to be a pragmatist, his interest in what was then the infant science of psychology compels him for very personal reasons to offer what might be called "consolations" and to substitute a psychological theory of truth for Peirce's demanding logical theory of meaning. The nature of the problems James dealt with in his comparative and historical studies into the varieties of religious experience perhaps caused him to be far more compassionate and sensitive to fallible human behavior and needs as he popularized pragmatism beyond the strict limits Peirce's theory of meaning could logically allow. For example, James believed in the existence of a personal God who was no mere convenient hypothesis. If a concept is true because of its consequences, then God is true, for he works, according to James. If he does not work for me, that is my misfortune; but he works for James and is true for him; and he could "care less" if my truth is different from his. Insofar as his will-to-believe satisfies his need and is essential to his well-being, James claims that it has the same degree of truth and has evidence equally as impressive as that which science can muster. James, then, is pluralistic and relativistic. He is convinced that there is no one best course of action or one absolute standard for measuring the truth of all propositions. Indeed, one may be a careful scientist and still believe in a God; one may believe in any one of the great religions of the world if he needs it and it will be true for him. This frank acknowledgment of the multitude of life-styles which is relative to the individual and his specific culture is usually condemned by subsequent pragmatists as being more liberal than the method of science can allow or tolerate. To James's view, we should not expect different tribes or nationalities to abandon what science might adjudge to be their unscientific beliefs. To strict pragmatists, this makes James "irrational" and "subjectivistic"; in fact, many have banned him from the movement and contemptuously labeled him "a mere existentialist."

To others, it is to the credit of James that he was intensely aware of the risk he was taking when he addressed himself to man's psychological if not metaphysical needs. He likewise insisted upon dealing with the "big" questions like the existence of God—which science cannot ask and cannot answer. Such a terrible question is important to many men in many lands and can and often does make a profound difference in the lives of those who attempt to answer it. James knew that "Naked Apes" have "practical" needs and metaphysical itches which science cannot scratch. James, for example, had a "practical" need to believe in the Christian God and the promises of that religion; and he "used" pragmatism to help him defend what was true for him. James is the most consistently humanistic of the great pragmatists, but he is currently "the odd man out" because he was not a consistently scientific humanist.

The real conflict between Peirce and James over what are "true" and what are "practical" means is staggering; for if James is representative man who uses science as it suits him, despite his training, and not otherwise, when he is presumably floating on his stream of consciousness, there can be no method and consequent criteria for the solution of mutual problems: "Everything is possible"; all things are relative, and it is futile and cruel to dream of the day when we all live in a world society of reflective problem solvers guided by their capacity for self-sacrifice and their undeviating integrity as conscientious, farsighted logical beings animated solely by the scientific spirit. It may be that those who attempt to disprove the pluralism and relativism of James and his "faith" in an attempt to bring him into harmony with the more consistently scientific Peirce and Dewey will one day have to make an embarrassed confession that the confidence they have in the scientific method to solve all human problems is equally a "matter of faith," not demonstrable by science itself, equally tenuous, and equally a matter of, "Well, we have to believe something and start somewhere."

It is John Dewey who is most often associated with the educational philosophy of pragmatism. No educational philosopher in history has been referred to more and understood less. He is still the major figure in American educational thought. What Paul is to Christianity, Plato to idealism, Aristotle to realism, and Robert Hutchins is to literary humanism, Dewey is to instrumentalism. Dewey has been constantly at the eye of the hurricane generated by pragmatism. His long and varied career resulted in an astonishing output of published materials. Academic lifetimes are spent studying the development of Dewey's thought. To lovers of grace and style, the writing of Dewey seems ponderous, wordy, redundant, and leaden; and this drives many a would-be reader to secondary commentaries of uneven worth.

Dewey spent much of his time fending off detractors and castigating others in education who he thought misunderstood his work or did things in practice not sanctioned by his writings; consequently, much of his work reflects the continuing "infield fighting" among the pragmatists. He wrote many an epistle to the warring sects within the movement warning them of their excessive narrowness or excessively broad interpretations of his basic point of view. To this day, splinter groups and new sects of pragmatists emerge and multiply. In order to disassociate himself from the puerile abuses supposedly associated with genuine pragmatism, he came to call himself first an instrumentalist and finally, and most accurately, an experimentalist. Regardless of the tag, many of the issues are the same. Literally tons of writings have been generated by Dewey's thought, so nothing that any single author now says about pragmatism—or if one prefers, instrumentalism, or experimentalism—goes unchallenged by other authorities within the movement. To one who has not yet been brought into the philosophy, it seems that those most competent to speak about it are often too involved in "family quarrels" about definition and theory to communicate with the teachers on the front line in the classroom where educational philosophy is put to the crucial test. With these reservations in mind, the safest comments about the philosophy would seem to be as follows.

In his earliest philosophical phase, Dewey—who has been described as the greatest of American philosophers—was an ardent Hegelian idealist. This was probably because of the influence of William Torrey Harris and George Sylvester Morris. During the first ten years of his college teaching (1884-94), Dewey moved from the idealist's camp to the beginning of a pragmatic philosophy which he was to characterize with the name of instrumentalism. This philosophy emphasizes the social function of intelligence, that ideas are instruments of living, rather than ends. Dewey regarded philosophy as a general theory of education, and placed a great deal of emphasis on epistemological and axiological considerations.

Pragmatism is basically an epistemological undertaking keynoted by its theory of truth and meaning. This theory that truth can be known only through its practical verifiable consequences and is a social matter of consensus based upon a scientific analysis of the evidence is best expressed by Dewey. This to Dewey's followers is proof of democracy in action and that an educated citizenry will evaluate the evidence scientifically and come to the logical solution of the particular problems. To many, this seems to be socialism in action.

In keeping with the view that epistemology is the most important, perhaps the only, traditional philosophical category that has any justification, the pragmatist holds that knowledge is rooted in experience, but experience may be immediate or mediated. Immediate experience is simply undergoing. Mediated experience is the interaction of man and his mind with his environment. It requires the use of intelligence. The process involved in the mediation of experience has been variously called the five-step thought process and the scientific method. What it amounts to are the following five steps. First is the vague uneasiness that lets us know we have a problem that has upset our equilibrium. Second is the refinement of the problem. This is the detailing of the problem, the bringing it into the light to take a look at it. Third is the forming of hypotheses or tentative solutions to the problem. Fourth is the considering of the consequences of various activities and the mental testing of alternative solutions. This is one of the most important steps, since it is here that the fifth step will be decided on. The fifth step in this process is the actual testing of our solution under so-called field conditions. This is where the results of our intelligence are applied. Now in many cases it will not matter if we have made a mistake. It will simply mean "back to the drawing board," and it is for this reason that many people underrate the importance of the fourth step in this process. But not all applications of a solution leave the alternatives in the fourth step open. It is quite possible that by taking a particular course of action we make it impossible to return to one of the roads not taken. It is for this reason that the fourth step places as great a moral burden on man's shoulders as does the fifth. Truth in this system can be viewed as the production of desired consequences through the five-step thought process. But this does not give truth a special existential status; it simply means that in a particular case something is true.

Truth may, therefore, exist in varying degrees. Truth is contingent on, or relative to, a set of circumstances. Knowing is an open-ended, on-going, human activity. As such it is constantly subject to error. There are three major points of significance to the pragmatic epistemology. First, it is an open-ended activity, open to the public and, in fact, dependent upon the public test rather than some private metaphysical test. Second, its conclusions are subject to error and are continuously being revised in terms of new conditions and new consequences. And third, it places the ultimate responsibility for truth and knowledge directly upon the shoulders of man. This is a tremendous responsibility and, of course, there are many who would prefer to shirk this responsibility and retreat to the security of a more authoritarian system.

As regards teaching methods, ethical values are a product of the transactional functioning of man and society. They are in no sense absolutes, and generalizations cannot be sanctioned except from the secular and naturalist point of departure. The good is that which resolves indeterminate situations in the best way possible. Thus, the use of the intellect in the solving of problems is considered good by the pragmatists. Values emerge from the process of reflective deliberation. But how do we know what is the best possible solution to a problem? Dewey finds, as the basis of all ethics, growth. That which contributes to growth is good. That which would stunt or deflect it is bad. But man is not an island unto himself. What may appear good in the private sense must also be explored in the public sense. We must ask two questions then about an act or decision. First, what are the individual consequences? And second, what are the public consequences? We must also consider whether these consequences will contribute to, or retard, growth. The major concern then, of pragmatic ethical theory, is the public test; the test that is open to the public and which can be reiterated or verified by others.

Pragmatists as a group have little to say about the nature of beauty, aesthetics. The pragmatist's standards of beauty differ from those of the other philosophies we have discussed in that they do not exist in some separate realm. What is beautiful is simply what we find to be beautiful in our individual experience. Art is simply a way in which an artist describes his own experiences to us. The public test is whether he has communicated this experience to us and whether others share the pleasure we receive from his work of art. Critics of pragmatism claim that such a view of art is superficial at best.

For the pragmatist, society is a process in which individuals participate. Society is the source from which people derive all that makes them individuals. It is from man's relationship to society that he derives his values. Society is a basic concept in contemporary pragmatism, since all actions must be considered in the light of their social consequences. The school, therefore, must be concerned with society and with its students as members of society. Pragmatism sees the school as vitally interested in, and concerned with, social change and teaching the adults of the future to deal with the planning necessarily involved in the process called society. Since this position strongly advocates wholehearted involvement in society by all citizens, and because it views group decision in the light of consequences as important, and because it places responsibility on the individual, it has been called a democratic philosophy. Obviously, great stress is placed upon the socialization of the child as well as his intellectual training.

Perhaps the best statement of what might be called the pragmatist's educational aims can be found in the writing of John Dewey. In *Democracy and Education* he wrote that education is "that reconstruction or reorganization of experience which adds to the meaning of experience, and which increases ability to direct the course of subsequent experience."* Thus, the aim of education that might be derived from this definition would include the helping of the child to develop in such a way as to contribute to his continuing growth. Dewey disliked the use of the term "aims," in its usual sense because it implied an end, and Dewey saw no final and permanent end to education. Education is continuous throughout life, fluid, dynamic, and open-ended.

Teachers and students alike ideally participate in the process of learning. Dewey is fond of saying that education is life, not preparation for it at some distant, future date. This, to the pragmatists, helps solve the motivation problem. Of course, the lecture method is damned because it makes the students passive receptors dependent upon the authority of the teacher rather than responsible to the problem at hand. (How many of us have listened respectfully to lengthy lectures about the evils of lecturing?) It follows that the subject per se has no intrinsic value; it is the method by which we solve the problems at hand that matters most; therefore, the most common method employed in the pragmatist's school will be the project method. Classroom discussion in a free and open atmosphere is encouraged, as well as individual problem-solving research. All of this may well involve a tremendous amount of reading, studying, and traditional subject-matter mastery. The problems on which education is centered, however, must be the real problems of the students, not problems from textbooks, or even problems thought up by the teacher which have a neat solution that he can reveal at the end of the exercise. The method is rooted in the psychological needs of the student rather than the logical order of the subject matter. Thus, method is nothing more than the helping of students to use intelligence and the scientific method in the solution of problems that are made meaningful to them.

*John Dewey, *Democracy and Education* (New York: Macmillan, 1916), pp. 89-90.

The subject matter of the pragmatist's curriculum in any educative program is any experience contributing to growth. The curriculum is not hindered by subject-matter lines, but rather it is divided into units which grow out of the questions and experiences of the learners. The curriculum is learner-centered; it changes and shifts as the needs of the learners vary. Subject matter per se and the traditional arrangements of subject matter are seen as an arbitrary and wasteful system to which all learners have been forced to conform. The pragmatist rejects this system in order to center the subject matter on the problems and needs of the learner.

This often necessitates team teaching and interdepartmental course offerings. Certainly, it would follow from this that a variety of electives and the opportunity for students to select independent study programs should be encouraged, since the needs, aptitudes, and abilities of students are so diverse. The school would not be run as a "tight ship" with which the administrator would have few logistic problems and automatic budgets. Learning experiences are provided for in media centers and the opportunities for students to grow through the informal, but supervised, extracurricular activities.

To the experimentalists, great confidence is placed on the student to use his freedom of choice wisely and seek out the options most meaningful to him. To them, the student will be more productive in a healthful, structured school environment which does not hold him captive to bells. The student is an experiencing organism capable of using intelligence to resolve his problems. The student is viewed as a whole organism involved in the experience which is the school. This whole organism consists of the biological child, the psychological child, and the social child. The experiencing organism that is the learner brings to school with him all the meanings, values, and experiences that constitute his personality, his self. Of course, the self evolves and finds new meanings and values as the techniques of problem solving are mastered.

For the effectiveness of pragmatism, the individual teacher in the classroom, which is a kind of laboratory where ideas are put to the test of the quality of the evidence as measured by the scientific method, is the most important element. Contrary to much public misunderstanding, this makes the difficult job of the teacher more demanding; he cannot simply structure materials to be presented at his convenience. If the classroom is a kind of marketplace or town forum, he must be prepared to answer questions or direct students to reliable sources which can help them solve the problems presented. The teacher then must be a competent, well informed resource to be used by the students. The teacher for the pragmatist is a member of the learning group who serves in the capacity of helper, guide, and arranger of experiences. He is as involved in the educative process as are his students. This does not mean that the teacher abdicates responsibility; just the opposite is true. The teacher is responsible for working with the students and helping them develop their own projects. He advises and directs projects and activities that arise out of the felt needs of the students rather than those of the teacher. He must arrange the conditions by, as Dewey indicates, simplifying, purifying, ordering, and balancing the environment in such a way as to provide the experiences that will contribute the most to the growth of his students. He embodies the correct application of problem-solving techniques. In such a view, the teacher is also a comrade and counselor whose task is not contained by four walls.

The ideas of advanced pragmatism, experimentalism, are not the product of Dewey's thinking alone. Dewey never intended, and his method never allowed, for his being assigned the role of the sun in the galaxy of ideas related to pragmatism. He did, however, denounce the excesses of those who professed to be working from his basic and germinal insights. The excesses of progressivism, which shares many of the same principles of genuine pragmatism but which minimized the place of subject matter mastery and the responsibilities of the classroom teacher, were disclaimed by him.

He also denounced much of an offshoot of pragmatism called reconstructionism. Reconstructionism is not basically different from pragmatism. It shares in much of pragmatic thought, and differs only in its emphatic social policy. Its most ardent spokesman is Theodore Brameld, who indicates that the major difference lies in the emphasis the reconstructionist places on philosophy in the cultural context. Philosophy is a tool, and as such, the reconstructionists say, should be used for more than just explaining experience. It must help build a better society. This, says the reconstructionist, is especially true in these days of cultural crisis. Intelligence must be used for more than just adjusting to our environment—it must be used to logically, carefully, and consistently build a better culture. And the place to begin is in the school.

Dewey regarded the reconstructionists as setting goals and ends for education which his open-ended method did not allow for. To set ends and predetermined social goals other than the principle of "growth" itself smacked too much of traditional philosophy to Dewey and seemed opposed to democratic self-determination. To Dewey it short-cut logical processes as Hegelianism had done and sanctioned final goals for education not justified by the experimental logic. For Dewey, such a view of the planned society seemed to imply a group of authoritarian planners whose choice of ends could not be verified in advance by the scientific, democratic method. Dewey regarded reconstructionism as a step backward, since the reconstructionists could no more justify their version of the nature of the values and plans of action to be realized than the traditional philosophers. To Dewey they seemed too anxious to remodel society to fit their own Utopian ideals. Further, though the reconstructionists made much of their dependence upon democracy, psychology, and the findings of the natural and social sciences, Dewey feared they would deduce behavior and curriculum from the arbitrary ends they had chosen to be realized, as if they were first principles. Dewey suspected that they were too shrill and impatient to remake society according to their own plan in a period of crises to be sufficiently scrupulous practitioners of the experimental method, which does not allow for prejudging the outcomes of investigation and scientific inquiry. In keeping with his distrust of system builders, Dewey and his followers disclaimed reconstructionism for providing a speculative "philosophical" frame of reference from which to view the educative process. Dewey suspected Reconstructionism might become a program of authoritarian and persuasive indoctrination rather than the method of intelligence and logic at work in an open democratic society committed to an investigation of evidence.

Though some claim scientific logical empiricism based largely upon careful linguistic analysis of terms used in education is a form of pragmatism, the analytic philosophers do not usually claim adherence to any school of systematic thought. What these free souls are committed to is an intense, minute analysis of the meanings — connotative and denotative, or lack of them — to be found in all writing related to education. Consequently, they examine terms to determine their vagueness or logical precision in the various contexts in which they appear. Needless to say, this is an advanced, technical study undertaken by scholars of vast erudition and broad reading backgrounds trained to be especially sensitive to and critical of our uses of logic and language. For some, this means ethical propositions are simply statements which index personal preferences to be logically analyzed.

The scientific empiricist designation covers a variety of different, but related, positions. What is common to all of them is their concern with questions of meaning in preference to questions of truth. The scientific empiricists point out that they are not concerned with questions inside a frame of reference, as in traditional philosophy, but rather with questions about the frame of reference. Many of this group deal with this problem through an analysis of language and its meaning. A. J. Ayer, for example, is particularly concerned with the meaning of sentences as opposed to individual words. Thus, the scientific empiricists are involved in a discourse about discourse. They do not stop here, however. They set up a criterion of verifiability to establish whether or not a statement has meaning. For Ayer, verifiability is whether or not a statement has meaning. He concedes that it does if it is logically possible to make observations relevant to the probability of its truth or falsehood. Some scientific empiricists go even further than Ayer, indicating that verifiability is nothing more than a logical lack of self-contradiction. Basically, the criterion of verifiability simply imputes meaning to statements that can be either verified or falsified. It is this criterion that leads to the scientific empiricists' denial of metaphysics. Thus the emphasis of the school, although not opposed to the mainstream of pragmatic thought, places its primary concern on the methodological aspects of epistemology.

Because they view their job to be the clarification of language in specific usages and instances or in their many different contexts, they make no pretension to being system builders. In effect, they are research scientists who examine terms like "teaching," "learning," "evaluation," or "accountability" microscopically under laboratory conditions. To some, these intent and concentrated scholars are a bother and pest; they are perceived as being sadistic lovers of verbal trivia who delight in puncturing the balloons of their more pretentious brethren. Such is not their intent; they perform a valuable and needed service, however unsettling, to writers about education. As one notorious example which infuriates strict experimentalists, they attempt to demonstrate that Dewey's use of the term "growth" is never adequately defined, vague when considered from its different textual contexts, and is, in effect, the mysterious "god" of his system. If they are correct, it indeed undermines the experimental position. Once again, the divisions of analytic "schools" do not pretend to be other than a valuable tool of equal worth and value to all adherents of different positions taken by educational thinkers. Understandably, the preoccupation of pragmatism with epistemology, clarity, precision, and logic has led many thinkers from that position to move to linguistic and logical analysis. Such thinkers come from a variety of academic backgrounds and perform a similar service for other academic disciplines.

Partly because pragmatism has had a troubled history marked by savage battles with its opponents and among its own members, it becomes increasingly difficult to separate what the movement "really is" from the heresies and departures from it. Further, self-designated pragmatists are not in agreement. To exponents of the other education philosophies, pragmatism often seems intolerant and dogmatically arrogant in its contempt for their views. Exponents of other schools of educational thought also suspect that despite its angry professed innocence, pragmatism is itself a "school" and a "system" which is equally prescriptive. To the existentialists especially, it seems the pragmatic movement has become reactionary, closed, and suspicious of all new ideas which do not fit neatly into its established theories. To some, it seems the movement has become viciously self-defensive and indignantly self-righteous. One of the more extreme charges heard increasingly from a variety of sources inside and outside of education is that pragmatism has become more concerned with theory and self-defense than its application and "growth." Indeed, it is even being suggested that pragmatism, though it may be most attractive in theory, has seldom been implemented because of its essential oversimplifications, optimism, and naivete about the contemporary world. It is suggested that pragmatism increasingly fails to live up to its brash claims and is no longer a viable philosophy as we confront a future radically different from the past. Of course, pragmatists deny all such allegations as being superficial misrepresentations of their view. Pragmatism is being confronted on all sides and is doing a remarkable job of defending itself against all critics as it argues that it will yet be the philosophy of the future. All, none, or some of the criticisms of pragmatism may be "true." It is up to the reader to decide this complex issue, for it cannot be evaded further. First, he should consider the existential perspectives which demonstrate why in its view genuine pragmatism as currently formulated may be difficult if not impossible in application. Of course, it may be that pragmatism may so redefine and clarify its position in this time of "crises of confidence" and "credibility gap" that it will continue to dominate and direct the enterprise of "doing" educational philosophy in North America.

SUGGESTED READINGS

AYER, ALFRED JULES. *Language, Truth, and Logic.* New York: Dover Publications, 1946. Here we have the basis for the rejection by logical positivists of metaphysics and *a priori* system building.

BRAMELD, THEODORE. *Education for the Emerging Age.* New York: Harper & Row, 1965. This is a basic primary source for those wanting to understand reconstructionism, especially for those sympathetic to the appeal to set a course of direction for modern education.

GRUBER, FREDRICK C. *Foundations for a Philosophy of Education.* New York: Thomas Crowell, 1961. The sympathetic account of pragmatism is extremely well thought out.

DEWEY, JOHN. *Democracy and Education.* New York: Macmillan, 1916. This work is essential for an understanding of how the pragmatists come to regard the method of science to be the best guarantee of a viable educational system in a democracy.

_____. *How We Think.* Chicago: Henry Regnery; A Gateway Paperback Edition, 1971. Here is a crucial argument by Dewey for rejecting past modes of thought in favor of reflective problem solving. It leaves no past philosophy of education unscathed.

_____. *Reconstruction in Philosophy.* New York: Mentor Books, 1950. This is an exciting, readable book which states Dewey's reasons for rejecting the sources from which, and methods by which, past philosophers solved their problems. He argues convincingly that philosophies must change with the ages which produce them. He makes of philosophy an active process as opposed to a means of passive resignation. It is a hopeful and essential book for those who would understand experimentalism.

LANCASTER, LANE W. *Masters of Political Thought,* Vol. 3. Boston: Houghton Mifflin [N.D.]. Lancaster examines the ideas of Dewey as they relate to political theory. Lancaster clearly states his reasons for holding that any speculative system which ignores the past and its modes of thinking is guilty of crudity and irrationalism and can only contribute to further frustration and confusion.

SMITH, JOHN E. *The Spirit of American Philosophy.* New York: Oxford University Press; A Galaxy Book, 1966. Though generally sympathetic to the development of pragmatism, Smith questions whether or not it has a sufficient sense of tragedy to attract adherents who do not share its optimistic assessments of men in action.

WYNNE, JOHN P. *Philosophies of Education from the Standpoint of the Philosophy of Experimentalism.* New York: Prentice-Hall, 1947. This is an extremely partisan account of why experimentalism is the only defensible educational philosophy. If one can endure the missionary zeal, it does dramatize why experimentalism is intolerant of other philosophical stances.

CHAPTER 5

The Challenge of Existentialism

Recently, and perhaps inadvertently, a controversy has emerged almost without warning in educational philosophy between the entrenched, latter-day pragmatists — who now prefer to be called experimentalists — and the existential thinkers who increasingly address themselves to the problems of education. Established academic philosophers of education from every camp have moved from their earlier positions to an exploration of the existential hypothesis, and books in educational philosophy written by existentialists multiply. There is an increasing number of existential thinkers being named to faculty positions in education. Ironically, although existential thinking is the latest movement in educational thinking, it has thus far more in common with the traditional philosophies and even indirectly with logical positivism than with pragmatism — which it would seem most to resemble.

Existentialism brings philosophy down to earth again for this age by reopening many of the essential problems of ethics to reinvestigation. Though other philosophies may protest the unwillingness of existentialism to become a system and develop a metaphysical frame of reference, they admire it for the quality and depth of the questions it poses for modern man. Like logical positivism and the schools of analysis, it confronts nonsense and the possibility that communication has broken down. It also rejects any notion that we can solve a problem by ignoring the specific context of the problem or a set of actions by neglecting the context in favor of restating favorite abstract theories.

Suddenly, influential writers are labeling and defining the increasing awareness of pragmatism and existentialism of each other to be a "confrontation."* Such commentators do not make it clear whether or not one of the philosophies will absorb the other in some

*Leroy F. Troutner, "The Confrontation Between Experimentalism and Existentialism," in *Philosophy for a New Generation* by A. K. Bierman and James A. Gould (London: Macmillan, 1970).

new synthesis or if there is some exclusive "either/or" choice to be made between them. It does seem, however, that the partisan exponents of one point of view or the other are often to be found defending their position at the expense of the other.

Such a confrontation could hardly have been anticipated even ten years ago, when there were very few established educational philosophers who were identified with existentialism; certainly, they would have not encountered a systematic analysis of the existential point of view as a part of their professional training to become educational philosophers. More commonly existentialism was a term used by students of the humanities who studied the rise of contemporary literature and continental philosophy; it is, indeed, a form of radical empiricism which traces out with ruthless logic what follows from a totally secular view of the world. Even liberal theologians of different religious persuasions with a variety of professional backgrounds were suddenly emerging as the existential proponents of an anti-dogmatic crises theology which threatened to destroy institutionalized religions and their remote Sunday Gods.

Until recently, those existential thinkers who did write about educational reform were seldom themselves professional educators or trained in the analytic rigors of the scientific approach to the problems of educational philosophy; consequently, their contributions, however exciting and provocative, tended to be fashionable superimpositions upon educational theory rather than genuine contributions to it. Existentialism was still thought to be a "mood" expressed by creative artists and Romantic, literary philosophers rather than a subtle and technical modern philosophy deserving of close investigation. To be an existentialist requires one to know his history, philosophy, literature, and logic; it is too stark and demanding a philosophy to be dismissed as a fad or affectation of Left Bank wine-bibers.

Even though this much has been conceded about the antecedents of existentialism prior to its systematic application to the problems of education by writers of varying quality and quantity, it is no longer possible to ignore the import of the existential impact on education, since more and more serious educational philosophers are writing from an existential point of view, reacting to it, or attempting to discredit the movement before it absorbs or discredits them. Even if there were no existential thinkers already in education, the influence and popularity of existential lore in the various literary and art forms, including cinema, would make such an application inevitable.

Textbooks in English with titles like *The Identity Crisis,* works in psychology like the one by Kenneth Kenniston entitled *The*

Uncommitted, and the dozens of books addressing themselves to the breakdown of human communication, community, and common purpose are clearly existential in theme. Certainly, the books of Desmond Morris about *The Naked Ape* and *The Human Zoo* and Toffler's work, *Future Shock,* also enforce the notion that man is, perhaps, more complex, irrational, and fragile than the exponents of the method of science as the sole model for human progress would have us imagine. If this is so, we can better understand why experimental theory seems so difficult—if not impossible—in application. In psychology, the gestalt thinkers and Carl Rogers as well as Rollo May, Robert Lindler, Carl Jung, and Karl Jaspers are easily identified as having close ties to existentialism. In sociology, transactional analysis is being given more credence. In comparative education we are told our favorite theories about education do not readily apply to the peoples of developing countries, who often and increasingly reject our scientific models for their educational reform and social progress. Everywhere in the social sciences, we find established theories being reassessed and fresh, unorthodox thinking to meet the new realities of crisis and change. The situation is so fluid and complex that some would say the social sciences are being ventilated by philosophical thought in order to become more reliable and relevant to the understanding of intricate problems.

Nowhere is the basis for this reaction to the rationalistic faith in the application of the methods of science as the sole guide for human betterment and the sole good from which all blessings flow more clearly expressed than by the existentialists, who suggest that the theories which we were to apply that would lead us to some secular Utopian planned society have not had the desired effects and have, perhaps, been largely responsible for the effects of such an impossible dream upon people. In sensitive and horrified protest against the apparent meaninglessness, shortsightedness, and absurdity of such a deterministic, impersonal order, the existentialist talks about how to reverse the trend away from estrangement, fragmentation, lost identities, lost communication, lost sense of unifying objectives, and the sense of absurdity and meaninglessness of life. Modern man has been cast adrift as science has destroyed his moorings; yet science has done little to provide a self-regulating gyroscope which will enable man to keep his balance or bend without breaking. Science has largely destroyed the continuity of life's experiences and made the compartmentalization, specialization, and incoherence of man's life into a principle at dreadful human cost. Thus, it turns out, that science has destroyed even the possibility of trusting science. Strip mining may be scientific and efficient, but it has mutilated man's spirit and destroyed his environment from West Virginia to New Caledonia.

Yet refining and employing the methods of science correctly requires specialization of a high order. It was inevitable for man to use science to gain some control over his environment, raise his material standard of living, relieve him from drudgery and back-breaking labor, enable him to increase the yields on his acreage, and find cures for ailments once thought hopeless. Many of the problems still confronting society, like choked traffic ways into the urban sprawl where men will work in even greater numbers, will be relieved by applying technology to provide efficient, dependable mass transit systems.

Science is one of the greatest tools of civilization, along with religion and art. But science is not and cannot be the god of men. Science itself has destroyed even the possibility of placing our full confidence in science in place of past absolutes, yet we have so misused the tool for immediate gain by ignoring the consequences of our greed, power-mongering, and short-run repairs, that science has been personified as an enemy. What we know about psychology and man's weaknesses and needs for status has been exploited by ad men and political campaign managers selling images rather than interchangeable products that are not necessarily any better than what we now have even though they are "new, chemically formulated, laboratory tested, scientific preparations containing 'opqurstuvwxyz'." Some hucksters are far better informed about psychology and consistent in its perverse applications than most educators are in its positive uses. The tools of science could be used to manufacture light bulbs that burn to the end of the century, construct low-cost housing, and assemble cars that run with bumpers that bump instead of planning cars that rust and are made to be obsolete and fall apart like the one-horse shay after a few short years. While business booms, the auto graveyards spread. In a few short years, we may finally develop a technology to mine our junk piles to make more junk. Science in no way commands that we be so dumb and foolish in our sense of values that we judge each other by how much we own, our power and prestige, or how much we earn.

Yet the seemingly irreversible advances of science have dislocated our lives and forced us to change, retool, and recycle ourselves. Our life patterns and values were changed more in the first half of the twentieth century than during all the centuries which preceded it and will change at even faster rates in the last half of this century. Autos, contraceptives, penicillin, radio, and television alone have vastly altered traditional moralities, and culture shock and cultural lag are the inevitable consequences. Small wonder that man experiences alienation as a way of life and fears that the god "Science" is the enemy. To some who project future possibilities on the basis of current trends, man is an endangered species reduced to an appendage to the impersonal machines that already work faster and better than they. Man fears his skills will become obsolete and that at any time he will have no basis for pride in work — or work to do as the machines "talk" to each other and breed new hybrid machines to create necessities nobody dreams of which displace more men. Man's sole task, so the argument goes, will be to consume the interchangeable glut of name-brand product beers, aspirins, tranquilizers, cigarettes, and guns mass-produced by machines until he dies of suffocation in his own litter with a whimpered goodby to "The Good Life." The alternative for others is the conviction that a "clean" nuclear bomb will bang us out of existence first. Such futilitarianism is suicidal and deserves either fate. There is an option.

The option is to realize that science is a neutral tool and method that man directs and controls to meet the ends he sets. In a world of "clean" bombs, it is time to dethrone the god we have made of science as if it had a vicious will of its own intent on destroying us. Science does not set goals. Men do and it is time to rethink some basic assumptions and the morality or lack of it which supports them, including naive assumptions about science.

In a time of possible overpopulation and depleted natural resources, even such basic assumptions as "growth" must be reassessed; for they are no longer supreme or intrinsic goods or self-justifying goals. To build livable communities, for example, it may be necessary to have a plan which limits even "growth." Terms like "quality of life" can no longer be ignored as unscientific primitivism as we face a future where more leisure will be available to greater segments of the public. If the public is willing to pay for clean air and water and relocate endangered species in lands closed to commercial development, it is a stance which reinstates ethical and aesthetic priorities. If most men are at some time unemployed in the future by new technologies, it is not for them to feel worthless or to feel ashamed; it is the leisure made possible by science that may civilize us at last.

Any philosophy which glosses over symptoms can hardly cure the diseases of modern life. If the society is also a reflection of education, as modern educators have insisted, we can hardly applaud many of the reflections of recent schooling. Alienation, fragmentation, job dissatisfaction, despair, alcoholism, disintegrating families, overflowing mental hospitals, war, arson, sniping, and dehumanization are everywhere apparent. Are these tragic effects not caused in part by educational programs which have not successfully enabled men to solve their identity problems and relate in meaningful ways to their various environments, each other, and themselves? We are, as Wordsworth said, "out of tune." By short-run problem solving directed to the solution of particular isolated malfunctions, we have raped the earth and destroyed the physical and social environment of man and created more problems than we have thus far solved. We must, it seems to the existentialists, weigh not only the material benefits, but also the long-range effects of our automation and technology, for example, upon the human condition. In our intellectual pride, we have gathered sufficient data about the moon to occupy teams of scientists for years, but we still know shockingly little about psychosomatic ailments or our dependence upon the oceans.

In self-defense, if nothing else, the experimentalists must refute the critics by restating their position more clearly and showing how the existential challenge to meet the future is not justified, since experimentalism will still reach its projected goals. It may be that the experimentalists will find ways to so define the basic psychological categories of existentialism that they too can be made a part of the scientific and systematic study of man without neglecting context or oversimplifying the very spirit of science itself.

This author would prefer to think that there is no need for a battle to the death between the two philosophies. Both have much to offer to awareness, insight, humanity, education, and to each other which can only be realized if they understand each other and find ways to work together. This means the existentialists, as literary humanists, will have to understand the confidence of those with the scientific outlook; and the experimentalists, as scientific humanists, will have to realize that the existentialists are not sophists, irrational articulate hippies, mere neurotics, or Romantics with an anti-scientific outlook. It is science gone mad, more impressed with putting stripes in toothpaste than finding ways to make the world inhabitable, that nauseates the existentialists by its absurdities. What madness to believe that a scientifically tested mouthwash or dancing lessons can restore man's confidence in himself and his world and enable him to find love, social acceptance, and an end to his "metaphysical" loneliness. We too rarely use the "method of intelligence" intelligently. Science is not a self-contained system and prescribes nothing; men, as "philosophers," must think and direct the valuable enterprise without neglecting its moral context.

To make the consequences of the scientific method, as verified by a non- or anti-scientific public, itself the arbiter of morality and aesthetics is the ultimate monstrous perversion of science. Such a notion presupposes that the scientific method is used to identify problems and that the public repeats the intellectual process and verifies the one true consequence. Most human beings do not even know what the scientific method is and could not apply it if they did. The results of such pseudo science confirm the vulgarities of a mass culture: "It is a scientifically proven fact that Norman Rockwell is a truer artist than El Greco and that Rod McKuen is a truer poet than Milton." The so-called public test of the verifiability of moral and aesthetic questions to determine values is less reliable than an opinion poll taken in a madhouse. By such a test Maoist China is "truer" than British socialism. To assume that the method of science functions with equal validity in the natural and social sciences also confirms the notion that the individual knows nothing and the god of science knows all and will reveal a miracle in time.

Existentialism, then, does not regard science as a god or a magic wand which automatically solves complex interrelated problems which cross "departmental lines." Rather than suppose that existentialism wants to be anti-scientific, it would be fairer to say that it wants a more honest, imaginative, responsible, and self-critical use of the scientific method, guided by an awareness of the fallibility of those who employ it. Social scientists, especially, must realize that their generalizations are temporary and do not have the universal applicability of the shifting physical laws of the natural sciences. Further, science alone cannot describe or solve all the needs and aspirations of the mass of living men. We are not merely computers and we have biological and affective needs equally as essential to our survival as our "intelligence."

Europe is the seed bed of existentialism. In Europe, the proud tower of vain intellectualism, vague idealism and slogans finally toppled in the First World War. The Europeans learned in agony that the world is a fragile place of crisis and perpetual transition. Yet the Americans gassed nauseously on about European decadence, a United States of Europe, and "the war to end all wars," so the world could be "made safe for democracy." American authors like Faulkner, who explored the depth of our human problems, were too long dismissed as "decadents" or "nihilists." Is it decadent or nihilistic or dishonorable to face our real problems squarely, refine them carefully, and go beyond despair to seek understandings and solutions which are not themselves misunderstandings or the genesis of further, more terrible problems? We must, in short, says the existentialist, anticipate problems and prepare for them rather than forever react too little and too late. Lake Erie died while thousands of scientists collected unemployment benefits. Educators are only now talking about the year-round school to help students understand a world vastly altered by the knowledge explosion, yet the school term is still based upon the needs of an agrarian society for children to work in the fields and help with the harvest.

The routine of many schools, with their assigned, bolted seats, still prepares students to enter a relatively stable industrial society already as remote from reality as the age of the pioneers. "Stop talking; it's time for speech class." "Put that turtle away, Jody, it's time for science; now turn to page 48 and color the dodo bird gray." Few medical schools talk about the morality of keeping patients with expensive terminal diseases alive or the option of alleviating suffering by allowing men to at least die with dignity. What we call "professionalism" is often an unethical conspiracy of silence. Every profession and every man is confronted in life with ethical dilemmas for which there are no rule-book answers or easy solutions, not even from science.

The method of science calls for a dispassionate review of the specific problem in isolation. It assesses often quite narrowly what it will accept in evidence. It too often overlooks the complexity of the evidence, the range of the problem, the fallibility of perception, the dangers at any point of going from the specifics we observe to generalizations which are too often then used as a basis for deducing what we ought to do in other cases, which may have only the most superficial of similarities. If experimental error has meaning it is not to discard significant variations from emerging patterns lest they deprive us of favorite oversimplifications. "That doesn't fit . . . out it goes. . . . Experimental error." Further, we cannot deny that the scientist is also a fallible, finite man with a colossal investment, human interest, and ego involvement in his work. Imagine the shock of the surgeon who declares a case to be hopeless and then sees the patient dancing and singing in the streets a week later after acupuncture. His choice of a method predetermined what he would see, how he would see it, and what the method predetermined the outcome to be. There are possibilities for problem solving far greater than any single method or frame of reference allows for. Witch doctors still effect miraculous cures in Africa.

In a world hungry for immediate solutions to overwhelming problems of terrifying priorities like the energy crisis and pollution, is it possible to urge a calm analysis of every problem, its distillation to manageable proportions by a team of scientists, each speaking a different technical language, an investigation of all the alternatives, possible effects, and conflicting reports before any attempt is made to formulate a hypothesis which might permanently solve that particular problem by a specific sequential plan of action? Further, if we make the test of the acceptance of the plan dependent upon public acceptance in a democracy with shockingly high rates of functional illiteracy and little comprehension of how scientists and science operate, the result may be based on everything but the evidence. Either the plan will be accepted because it means jobs or rejected because of the propaganda circulated by environmental groups, no member of which could read with comprehension the scientific evidence. In the meantime, the "patient" dies of neglect. The proposed solution may not have solved the problem if it were given the opportunity.

Clearly, urgent problems cannot wait indefinitely for distant "payoffs" which are at best gamblers' hopes, given the complexity of the problems and the number of things we didn't think about, predict, or consider as possibilities, since we are dealing with the dynamics of pulsing life, not laboratory models operating under ideal controlled conditions. In the decade just past and full of talk, theory conventions, seminars, sensitivity sessions, rap sessions, and "educational task forces," overdue reform of higher education came about as a consequence of burning libraries, occupied buildings, tragic deaths, and public backlash — not from education itself and its pompous expertise and feudal medieval orders. While the problems were pondered and researched and published, of course, the fuse burned and the organizational dry rot ignited. By the time the specific problems were even refined, they multiplied like Topsy; more problems were created by the delay and the evidence so carefully compiled was obsolete before it burned in the fires of the administration building. Among other things, the youths were trying to tell us that their emotional and biological needs were not welcome at college. They might also have been telling us that the hallowed curriculums of the "Establishment" are largely dysfunctional, out of joint. The students did not have tenure; they had to acquire skills relevant to their future in school or be obsolete the first day on their jobs after graduation. Academia, to them, had become a vacuum untouched by the problems and the demands of the real world.

A startling best-selling book by David Halberstam, who spent three years writing it, is called *The Best and the Brightest*. It illustrates dramatically how those few men who supposedly knew the Vietnam tragedy best, were trained to cope with it, and solve it never understood the complexity of the problem, the evidence, the meaning of it, or what to do on the basis of it. Their plans and theories did not work because the cultural diversity of the area did not allow for the United States to superimpose its values and methods upon a world governed by neither its values, its methods, its predictabilities, nor its needs. Presidents do not have a monopoly on being right or wrong. There is no longer time available to the superintendent of schools or departmental chairman to compile all of what he hopes is the relevant evidence, sort and assess it from every angle after consultation with elected committees before acting on staffing changes for the coming school year. Whatever decision he makes will antagonize somebody just as conscientious as himself. To delay or evade the decision is to compound the problem. At some point, the buck stops; and we cannot always know whether our decisions are correct. Sometimes, it may be better to make wrong decisions when a decision is urgent than to make a "right" decision too late. This is the existential point—where the buck stops and a man takes his stand. He takes his stand without the certainties of a Martin Luther, and he can never be sure whether or not he viewed the problem correctly, since he chose the point of view by which he judged the action and weighed the evidence. No point of view, including the scientific point of view, guarantees either the outcome or the validity of the outcome. Whatever happens, the existential man takes full responsibility and does not blame the point of view, the evidence, or his unfortunate childhood for the consequences which he bears manfully. No one could make the decision for him; he was condemned to the freedom to make the choice. Our recent Presidents were, in this profound sense, existential men. They were all tragically immersed in the same problem largely caused by our national vanity and unwillingness to leave other countries, cultures, religions, forms of government, and civilizations "unliberated" by our scientific rationalism. All ideologies ultimately prefer to kill or be killed rather than to live and let live. The Presidents were as alone in the White House as was Lincoln in his stocking feet pacing the halls, as they too faced a world of constant crisis and challenging kinds of change for which historical, metaphysical, or scientific precedents for solutions did not exist. Even if a precedent did exist, it might not work for a Vietnam. Humility, tolerance, and the final understanding by Americans that they are fallible, finite men, whatever methods they choose or organizations they join to escape from the agonizing responsibility for making ethical choices and living with the consequences, may be the "lesson" of Vietnam. It is the crux of existentialism that all ideologies are killers of thoughts if not of men. If we walk now in the rubble of our proud tower choking on the dust, we are at least once again realizing our share of what the existentialists call "the human condition," from which no one is exempt. This rediscovery of our fallibility and mortality, the universal tragedy, and the burden it places upon us makes us responsible for what we do with our science and our lives. Our lives precede any meanings we assign. Our existence is existentialism. For the existentialist, this is the challenge and there is "no exiting" from it for any of us. The existentialists, as individualists, protest a world in which men disregard human freedom and dignity again in the name of gods, essences, first principles, or for any "cause," including "science" and "progress."

The question inevitably arises as to how the existentialist defends his choice of values if there are no essences, absolutes, or consistently reliable generalizations, and the charge is made that he is a thrill-seeking hedonist who uses his "philosophy" as an excuse to do as he damn pleases. Existentialists have only a shared concern about the importance of making choices related to the all-too-human ethical dilemmas of specific men in specific action rather than a single shared method, articles of faith, or completed system to guide them. Because of this insistence upon the inescapable human responsibility to make commitments and ethical choices for which the existing guidelines do not always provide a clear course of action, it is what goes into the choice that is crucial, not solely its private or public consequences or even the motives. Certainly, Captain Billy Mitchell knew he faced a court-martial for presenting the evidence for air power. In that case, he was ultimately rewarded by the same public that rejected him earlier; but the act he performed was not done for selfish motives or the hope of reward. A pilot in Vietnam who refused to bomb populated cities like Hanoi was finished in the Air Force and knew it. The Nuremberg Trials established that crimes against humanity could not be justified by the excuse of "following orders." The newspaperman who refuses to reveal his sources and goes to jail for it lest he violate the principle of freedom of the press is equally as existential as a Socrates. The governmental employee who reveals waste and inefficiency in the Defense Department despite orders to conceal the evidence reinstates the principle of honesty in government.

None of the examples cited, and they can be multiplied a thousand times a day, is capricious, hedonistic, or self-seeking. The existential philosophy is what we do with our lives, not an abstract theory or a scoreboard tally of its private and public consequences. Truth was a reality when Socrates cross-examined the jury at Athens and consequently condemned himself. Freedom of the press existed when reporters defended it with an indeterminate jail sentence for remaining silent when directed to reveal news sources. Kindness exists when we help a friend or enemy in trouble, regardless of any prudential consideration of consequences. It is by our acts as much or more than our frequently hollow words that compassion is defined. In each case the model of the action affects others who must follow or reject it, but the act is the statement. A woman with two children and whose husband recently died in an automobile crash contemplating abortion makes her statement by her decision; but she does not expect other women in different circumstances to make the same choice. A man whose wife is ill or handicapped may seek voluntary sterilization, but this does not compel his best friends to do the same. A couple with several children may decide to raise a Latin American orphan rather than have more children of their own. A young man with a hatred for killing may refuse conscription and face the consequences for his choice. In a sense, all such acts are arbitrary and indefensible and cannot be adequately measured by public opinion polls or the scientific method.

Man realizes a non-social value like reading a book not because it is a problem-solving value or has public consequences, but because it is to him a personal joy. It is possible that none of the scales we use weigh accurately. If so, relativism and pluralism are inevitable and, perhaps, desirable; not all men should be melted in the same pot. In such a view, when we honor laws we do so out of support for them, not fear of punishment. When we abide by a majority decision, it is an act of voluntary assent which reinforces how we agree to be governed. Whenever we assign meaning to the evidence for — say — a zoning change and accept or reject the proposition, we also accept all the risks and perils that go with the choosing our point of view and making our decision. No matter what choice is made in the specific case, the possibility exists that it may be wrong. Is this not genuine experimentalism which is ethically responsible? Democracy guarantees us the right to be different and the right to be wrong. If we are wrong and know it, we can't blame the theory or anything else for our mistake or the damage it may have done to others; we can only apologize, rectify the harm if possible, reverse our course of action and vow not to make the same mistake again. People who cannot tolerate error can hardly tolerate people or the world.

Christian existentialists especially would say the value arena need not be such a nervous place. They would argue that it would make the sufferings of a Job intolerable. Yet the Christian existentialist sanctions plagues, earthquakes, and gas chambers by neglecting their context and the horrible meaninglessness of the disasters. The Christian denies the evidence and glorifies absurdity by "a leap of faith" which makes him a Christian, not an existentialist. Henceforth, he will know what to do and why. If a man embraces any finished system of thought or ideology or supernatural religion, he has agreed to stop thinking and to relate to theory rather than to life and fact. For example, God asked Abraham to sacrifice his favorite son as proof of love for Him. The atheistic existentialist would not sacrifice his son or his logic to any god. Man is more important than God. One can act out the Christian ethic by choosing to be merciful, for example, without buying the whole package of beliefs which predetermine subsequent choices. A God who could devise such a terrible test deserves killing, not worship. To worship the gods or first principles of any school of thought is ultimately irrational and causes us to oversimplify the evidence or discount the importance of the life of someone's favorite son. One can endure pain stoically with resignation without "buying" Stoicism. For all this, the atheistic existentialist understands and respects the gods of other men and the gods of academic and educational philosophers. All the atheistic and humanistic philosopher asks at this point is to be tolerated, allowed to describe the world he sees, and make his anguished decisions in "fear and trembling." His systematic doubt compels him to be an eclectic on the principle of rejecting all absolutes.

Amazingly, the existential educator shares much with the view of the pragmatist of the student as learner and would also work from the base of psychology and sociology. The existential educator would allow for play and physical activity, not because they build character, but because they exercise muscles, relieve tensions, and meet physical needs for spontaneous and joyful natural experiences. It is doubtful that the existentialist would destroy sports and the joy of play by forming leagues and teams and professionalizing a few so the others could watch. Playing, not winning or losing, would be the sole rationale. It meets a physical need.

The existentialist would probably not always work from the level of his students; very possibly he would require them to broaden their perspectives and stretch their minds by learning of the diversity of cultural patterns and life-styles rather than praising their provincialism. No doubt there would be much role playing and perhaps even psycho-drama. Textual materials in literature, for example, would encourage the student to consider who he is and who he would choose to be. Similarly, he would have to choose the values that go with being an authentic, unique, individual person with private as well as public needs. To answer such problems, the student would have a broad curriculum which would include some rough, hard academic subjects like

English so he could learn to articulate his needs, thoughts, and feelings and organize the complex world into manageable symbols. If the student could not articulate except with his fists or a gun, his opportunity to evolve into a relatively free person with the choice of options for a career is already shut off.

Science would also be stressed, but the student would "do" science and perform its operations very self-consciously, observing the scientific method in operation rather than just memorizing charts. Students would also be encouraged to understand the logic of science and the uses of logic in the critical analysis of language. As a part of science, students would learn to distinguish between opinion and argument and between straight logical thinking and the cheap psychological appeals that will be made to sell them everything from hula hoops to Presidents. The varied and required science curriculum would also be structured so students could cope with the hard world they would enter and not experience it as total disunity and incoherence. The world would seem less threatening to them than it does now to most college freshmen or seniors.

In areas designed specifically for the aesthetic and affective non-cognitive needs of children soon to be faced with leisure as adults, time would be provided in the schedule for children to hear and make music, dance, watch flowers grow, play with animals, paint, read, or watch nature films made by a Disney or Cousteau. On occasion, the teacher could read to the students or the students could read aloud for others. Opportunities to putter with clay and other substances would be essential. Opportunities to prepare and eat foods from other societies would be provided so students could develop all their senses to the fullest. In such an area, the worlds of poetry and world religions and art could be enjoyed for their healthy and sensitive or angry response to the worlds which produced them. The students would understand that art is not an argument for a particular method of viewing the world, but a way of expressing how man reacts to his many worlds. The ideal field trip would be a camping and hiking expedition. The student who completed such a system might be an authentic, functioning, self-disciplined person who could survive physically, psychologically, and "intellectually" in the worlds which are his to inhabit. Though the existential teacher's methods would share much in common with his pragmatic counterparts, the existentialists might be more directive in teaching skills and encouraging controversial dialog based on the course materials rather than endless "bull sessions" that pass for class discussion. The importance of the individual and his capacity for making responsible decisions would be stressed rather than "togetherness." The student would learn how to cope with defending his choices. Because the subject matter is important, a student might fail; but he would learn how to accept the failure and overcome it. Healthy self-fulfilling individuals equipped to meet their needs and respect the needs and abilities of others would "pay off" for such an educational view when such students functioned in a society with fewer social problems than ours.

It would be tragic if existentialism and experimentalism did not consider a synthesis or merger. Certainly terms like "alienation" can be scientifically defined to the satisfaction of experimentalists, their causes identified, and their effects measured. An enlightened experimentalism capable of self-criticism could synthesize its own point of view with the all-too-obvious existential agony. If experimentalism ignores the evidence of, or understandable human dimensions of, the existential situation as vague or unscientific, it cannot hope to survive except as a part of the saber-toothed, graduate school set of required courses — a training for obsolescence rather than the orderly planning it professes. It will become a disservice rather than a service to education. As eclectics and generalists, educational existentialists would not insist that those working together to solve a problem first agree in theory. Problems solved in theory only remain problems in theory. Maybe, it is the theory that is wrong.

What may be needed instead of elaborate intellectual rationales and plans which solve only problems in intellectual logic is the fuller realization that what we are meeting to implement are complex human needs wider than intellectual, preset goals impossible of realization or found to be empty upon realization. If men of all philosophical persuasions agree to try to identify the complex of human needs not being fully met by current education, then the scientists can devise reliable modes of measuring how well human beings are meeting their present and future human needs rather than how well they are conforming to an unreasonable rationalistic model devised in such a way that it cannot explore possibilities and solve human problems in a satisfying human way. It may be better to do what is possible, including compromise in life situations, than accomplish nothing because the plans and goals set are so abstract and dehumanized or absolute that the problems and their possible solutions are in effect ignored or rejected.

What we have, then, is no mere "scholastic controversy" being fought out by rival bands of academic monks. The direction of future educational objectives and programs hangs in the balance if there is no honest dialog based on mutual respect for the strengths of each position by the other and mutual tolerance for the weaknesses of each based on understanding. The problem of relating existentialism and experimentalism is further complicated when we realize that there are adherents of each school of thought in name only, the superficial "joiners" within the movements. There is considerable disagreement among the members about basic issues. Further, existentialism in education is young and not yet toughened to battle like the wily veteran experimentalism. Further, those articulate and careful apologists for their own philosophical position seem reluctant to meet the challenge of absorbing new ideas or revising pet notions. If the points of view drift farther apart they will inevitably become dogmatic and compel the exclusive allegiance of their camp followers.

If, on the other hand, there are grounds for some future synthesis of experimentalism and existentialism — as the author hypothesizes — some suggestions can be made about how it might come about and what might be gained in heightened sensitivity to the human predicament in a shattered world of flux and change. If an enlightened and imaginative use of the scientific method can help us understand and solve the increasing problems of fragmented and alienated men who must cope with ever more dizzying change in a post-technological society, it will do so by incorporating new materials for study into itself. By emphasizing the vital aspects of each of the philosophical "schools" alongside the other, we can hypothesize that we may have an input and understanding which we could not get by continuing to look at each in isolation from the other. Existentialists should be willing to consider ways of becoming more scientific in their description and analysis of the evidence for their descriptive point of view. If experimentalism persists in supposing that all existentialists are automatically anti-scientific and irrational, mere "philosophers," experimentalism will pass into the history books. Existentialism is closer to life, to current thought in the arts — largely ignored by the experimentalists — and the developments and fresh thinking "boiling" in the physical and social sciences. Indeed, existentialism may be more consistently scientific in outlook and adept at human problem solving for human needs, but not at supplying rationalizations for a defunct and fallible theory.

At this point, existentialism may offer more promise for the future of educational thought than experimentalism. For experimentalism to reject existentialism in favor of restating its obsolete theories based on naive assumption is to seal its own tomb. This would be indeed tragic, for all the philosophies are needed to work together to meet the challenge of philosophic goal setting and scientific measurements of our efforts toward self-transcendence. The scientific philosophers would by such an operation regain humility about the uses and limitations of science and a long-ranged view unlike the hubris they now tend to display, and the existentialists would become comrades addressing themselves to "real" problems as reflected even in works of art amenable to analysis by the dynamic and workable scientific method directed by their sensitive ethical and aesthetic considerations of the moral questions of philosophy and the ends and values men choose to honor.

SUGGESTED READINGS

Not all of the books listed are by existentialists or about it, but they all dramatize the cogency of existentialism to current problems and help one to understand the existential mood.

BARNES, HAZEL E. *An Existential Ethic.* New York: Vintage Books; A Division of Random House, 1971. Miss Barnes answers the critics who say existentialism is a wholly private affair without a social ethic. Her chapter on education (Chapter 9) is especially urgent. In part, she argues that education must provide students with the skills and abilities to become what they want to be and to make realistic choices based on self-knowledge.

BARRETT, WILLIAM. *Irrational Man.* Garden City, N.Y.: Doubleday Anchor Books A321, 1962. Barrett shows why irrational men cannot solve problems by superimposing rational, but unreasonable solutions upon complex problems and peoples. In his view, intellectual oversimplifications leave man's psychological, physical, and non-cognitive needs out of their theories and blueprints.

GREENE, MARJORIE. *Dreadful Freedom.* Chicago: University of Chicago Press, 1948. The primary value of Greene's book is the point-by-point comparison and contrast of experimentalism and existentialism side by side. It gets to the heart of the technical philosophical issues dividing the points of view which too often set them at cross-purposes.

HARRINGTON, ALAN. *Life in the Crystal Palace.* New York: Avon Riscus Edition, 1967. Harrington rejects the sham values and lack of authentic selfhood that are part of the anxiety of being part of a huge corporation. He rejects impersonal organized Utopianism.

KARL, FREDRICK R., and LEO HAMALIAN (eds.). *The Existential Imagination.* 1963. The introduction is a non-technical discussion of key elements and themes in existential thought. The literary selections dating to Shakespeare dramatize existential situations and show why literature is the most natural way of presenting existential materials. In such literature, thought has a specific context which the existentialist does not gloss over by superimposing theoretical generalizations which do not fit the specific problem.

KAUFMAN, WALTER (editor and contributor). *Existentialism from Dostoevsky to Sartre*. Cleveland, Ohio: Meridian Books M39, 1965. The many books by Kaufman are the best consistent account by an American of existentialism. Many would hope that Kaufman would address himself specifically to educational problems.

KAUFMAN, WALTER. *The Faith of a Heretic*. Garden City, N.Y.: A Doubleday Anchor Book A336, 1963. Here is a very personal account by Kaufman of how he came to reject alternatives to existentialism and why he does not regard it as a hopeless philosophy of gloom and despair. He perceives existentialism to be an on-going liberal education with lucidity as the aim.

KNELLER, GEORGE. *Existentialism and Education*. New York: Philosophical Library, 1958. This earliest of books about the relationship of existentialism to education is still one of the best and most readable. Kneller proposes a basis for viewing educational problems and specific courses of action.

_____. *Introduction to the Philosophy of Education*. New York: John Wiley, 1964. The text is keen in its analysis of all schools of educational thought, especially existentialism and logical analysis. It shows how both sets of thinkers look at problems first and frames of reference only after the problems have been defined. Kneller writes increasingly from the existential perspective.

LUBAC, HENRI, DE, S.J. *The Drama of Atheistic Humanism*. New York: Meridian Books M165. Jesuit priest Lubac provides a profound analysis of major existential thinkers with insight and understanding, but he no more accepts their conclusions as final than Aquinas accepted Aristotle.

MARCEL, GABRIEL. *The Philosophy of Existentialism*. New York: Citadel Press, 1961. Marcel is one of the world's foremost Catholic existentialists.

MICHAELSON, MICHAEL (ed.). *Christianity and the Existentialists*, New York: Charles Scribner Studies in Contemporary Theology, 1956. Michaelson and the authors of the essays he includes show how existentialists describe the world. For those who choose to prescribe what to do about the situation described, there are chapters on its relationships to Marxism, prescriptive schools of thought, especially Christian thought as a way of putting the existential view "in perspective."

MORRIS, DESMOND. *The Human Zoo*. Great Britain: A Coogi Book, 1971. Morris examines collective life and makes an interesting case for man's non-intellectual needs.

MORRIS, VAN CLEVE. *Existentialism in Education*. New York: Harper & Row, 1966. Van Cleve Morris is the best known and most often mentioned American philosopher of education writing consistently from an existential point of view.

TOFFLER, ALVIN. *Future Shock*. New York: Bantam Books, 1971. Though Toffler refuses to identify himself with "murky" existentialism, his work is a way of viewing the issues between experimentalism and existentialism. This book is "must" reading.

CHAPTER 6

You and Your Philosophy of Education

Though it may seem at first that there are as many philosophies of education as there are educational philosophies, it is possible to view the range of philosophies of education and discover that they do have some common ground. Each philosophy to be a philosophy can ultimately be reduced to a perception or a statement of how vast or limited is the world of man and the universe to which he relates. Once this is established, a statement is usually made about how man "should" relate to the reality of the world as described and accepted by him. This is done by providing a blueprint of how man should act to relate meaningfully and purposefully to the given situation. That the blueprint is reliable is the faith of the philosopher.

This may mean, as it does in the traditional philosophies, that the task of man is to conform to the ultimate reality, since it is "finished" in the sense that to discover the reality is already to answer all the meaningful questions about problems, values, and aims. In such a case, the system of thought is closed, and man's job is finished when he lives in harmony with the directives and prescriptions outside himself that are built into understanding such an ultimate reality; the goal then, is to conform, to understand, and to accept this pattern for the good life. Once this is done, the individual ceases from restless, vain, Faustian striving and accepts passively the impersonal "rules of the game" he chooses to play.

For the idealists, for example, the ultimate reality is non-material and mental; and the model of ideal behavior is to so rise above the deceptive, busy, confused physical world of practical problems and leisurely to contemplate the truth and beauty of the universal ideals which reveal themselves to be identically the same for all men in all times, places, and circumstances. Such an aristocratic view usually only develops in societies where some men are freed from physical labor. Frequently, the philosopher of this sort gains his retirement because there is a rigid class system where slaves do the work of the

83

mundane physical world. Almost equally as frequently, such a society is directed by the masters, or philosopher-kings, who alone have the big picture and therefore direct the activities of lesser men. To some, this is fascism; and it is always with us in military dictatorships which are often, to the view of the dictator and the dictated, affectionately conceived of as being for the good of all. Such plans often provide for social unity and a shared sense of direction by the citizens; in this sense, a Tito is equally as much the fatherly philosopher-king as a Mao, whose holy works include "The Little Red Book." The ruler is in effect the embodiment of the conscience of his people and can define right and wrong for them. Whatever the ruler says must be accepted, since it is in the best interests of the governed. Such idealism confronts all, for it is not individualistic and does not require hard original choices for anyone. Needless to say, such a system perpetuates itself largely through rigorous education. It calls for a bureaucracy with well defined chains of command.

The realists also agree that there are timeless universal truths which describe the nature of the world; but they can be discovered and honored by *all* men—not just the rulers—regardless of epoch, station in life, or circumstance. The great truths of the Enlightenment about the equality of all men and the belief in purpose, order, and meaningful progress might be a part of a view of reality. Needless to say, such a set of assumptions might be shared by all men living under a variety of forms of government and serve as a social cohesive—as they would in an ideal democracy. But the realist is also a man of action and does not make the end of life to be the contemplation of such shared absolutes. To him, there is the independent physical world of man in all its complexity in which man must live, and suffer, and die. Man can understand this world by describing it and bringing it into closer harmony with his physical needs by dominating it for his own purposes by building cities, specializing labor, domesticating animals, and by building dams and irrigation canals to bring the forces of nature under his domination.

In a sense, then, such a man is a dualist; he believes in at least two levels of reality equally as important, but not necessarily interrelated. Such men can compartmentalize their lives and even, perhaps, operate under two different, and not necessarily related, sets of realities. To meet their need to conform to the realities which transcend nature, such men often accept the guidance of the precepts of the dominant religion or set of traditions common to their culture; to meet their physical needs in the real world of bills and taxes, they engage in a variety of activities dependent upon their relationships to the physical world which determines the limits of how much freedom they have. In a sense, the American society is still partly realistic in this sense. Such things as the work ethic were once a reality for the vast majority of citizens; to this day, the realities of the different religions are not questioned or examined in the public schools and the principle of tolerance guides the teacher away from judging or allowing students to judge of the reality of the faith of the Eighth Day Adventists or Captain Billy Marvel's Witnesses. Such a society often operates efficiently because of the division of reality into separate or, for some, interdependent layers of reality.

Lest we scoff, we should realize that it was and is a remarkable accomplishment for man to so reduce the complexity of the universe in which he lives to only two sets of assumptions — moral and physical — which explain everything to him. How much easier it would be to believe, as the early Greeks did, for example, that each phenomenon in nature or human emotion and ideal was directly controlled by some god temporarily in ascendancy by having a tug of war with other gods or that he had been listening to our prayer to him (or her). If we read horoscopes, we may still fancy on a given day that the god of love or luck is on our side. Quite frequently, then, the realist accepts without question the validity of generalizations about truths which cannot be supported or rejected on the basis of any material evidence; at the same time, he is left free to argue about, describe, organize, weigh, analyze, and direct the physical substances of his material environment. He has, in effect, the best of two worlds.

The perennialist is like both the idealist and the realists; for he believes like the idealist in a purposeful, planned universe, guided by supernatural ideals. To him these ideals are spiritual realities which God devised for the protection of, and guidance of, his flock; such ideals are assented to by man in awe and worship and gratitude; for they assume that behind, above, and beyond the apparent disorder, strife, suffering, and incongruity of man's physical life, moral laws operate with strict cause and effect which assume that all is really for the best. No sparrow falls or child dies without a cause which we may not comprehend, but must accept. If we cannot accept or be in devotion to such a divine and mysterious set of operations, it is proof of our egoism, shortsightedness, and the depth to which we have become fallen, sinful creatures immersed in the apparent evils of the world. By such a view, it should not surprise us that the world is seen as being a less than perfect place, a place of trial and testing, of pain and suffering to be passively endured as proof of our worthiness of the love of God. It is folly to take our directions from such an imperfect world and its secular demands or the vain and sham rewards it offers to those who ignore their primary allegiance to a higher law and a higher order. Likewise, we must suffer much and endure meekly the indignities which are meted out to us in such a world, for heaven is our destination and earth is not our home.

The consolations of such views held in common to varying degrees by different religions have sustained millions in our history to endure cruelty, oppression, inequality, natural disasters, and abuse which they could not cope with otherwise. Such passivity does not encourage a man to regulate or manipulate his environment and strive to attain secular goals in this temporary, imperfect life. This fatalism is still a distinguishing characteristic of undeveloped countries and it is a value to them, for it enables them to endure the otherwise unendurable and justify the otherwise unjustifiable lot which is often their lives. Though such a view is thought to be realistic, it is still often otherworldly, and many men do operate in accordance with supernatural directives behind and beyond time and history more important to them than the things of this world or the superficial, deceptive, temptations of progress. To an extent, most men are still fatalistic in some sense: "You can't fight city hall." "That's the way the ball bounces." "Life is a lottery." "When your number is up, it's up," we say as we board planes that will whisk us to distant places at 600 miles an hour at 30,000 feet.

All of the systems too briefly reviewed to be wholly accurate thus far are, then, systems which explain everything we need to know about the world, how we ought to relate to it, and what we can do, if anything, to change it. All of the systems show how man is a part of the organic whole of the universe and that he is not alone, for what he ought to do with his life and how he should relate to the world and others are already prescribed for him and all others by the shared, given human essence which antedates his short existence on earth. To be honest with ourselves might compel most of us to realize to what extent our current world view is a compound of all the traditional views thus far described and more. We are still a kind of riddle to ourselves because we believe so many different kinds of propositions about ourselves which are contradictory. Until we become philosophers capable of understanding if not resolving these contradictions, our responses to life are likely to be inconsistent, without assurance, and subject to constant reassessment. If such is the case, the teacher is a greater force for both good and evil than it is comfortable to contemplate.

Confronting this understandable predicament the modern philosopher of education reviews the questions of the traditional philosophers and the variety of answers they found. He rejects the ideal of a closed, or finished, system which prescribes in advance how man should operate. The future is open and men can determine it by the choices they make. Man has no predetermined essence. To the pragmatist, to simply relive any one or all of the past philosophies is to spin wheels and get nowhere. The pragmatist proposed that they were all wrong and misdirected, for they are based on false dualisms, like mind versus emotion. Obviously, to him, they got nowhere and are equally indefensible. To be realistic, we must forget all such nonsense, for it is futile and gets us nowhere except deeper in the metaphysical mud. It is only the physical and social world as it can be described and refined by the method of science that has any meaning for man. It is only by using the method of science that measurable progress has been made; consequently, it is only within the framework of science and its strict reduction of experience to what can be measured quantitatively that meaningful questions can be asked, reliable methods of investigation used, and reliable conclusions reached.

Since philosophers have only confused the issues in the past, the philosopher to be reliable and of any value must operate with the same objectivity and detachment as the scientist. He must identify problems, apply scientific methodology, and produce the predicted consequences beyond question—which can be verified by all trained to evaluate the evidence. He must, of course, explain to others why this is the only sensible course of action and forever resist those, past and present, who insist upon asking absurd questions and following unreliable methods of investigation and their inconclusive, therefore damaging, results. This means that philosophical questions and modes of answering them are unscientific, unjustifiable, and unworthy of man's efforts. There is no concept—even honor or dignity—which has a universal status, and each situation and problem implies its own solution. It is in the material world that all our problems originate; they are compounded by the temptation of the mass of men to accept some unreliable and misleading statement or solution composed by past or present philosophers, religious thinkers, or artists—none of whom is scientific or reliable. The task of the philosopher, then, is to find ways of applying the technique of reflective problem solving which has unquestionably resulted in so much new knowledge and progress in the physical sciences to the problems of society, including education.

Once the method is understood as the only method of intelligence and taught to the exclusion of other methods of investigation except as examples of fallacies in the schools, the speculative underbrush can be cleared away and the real problems can be realistically refined, realistically solved by the method, and realistically finished so we can go on to other real problems which arise in the physical and social environment of man and require similar attention. In such a way, the philosopher performs a needed service and method for the resolution of problems unsolvable by any other technique. Ideally, such a program makes for progress and growth and the continuation of an evolving dynamic democracy. The task is not to create problems, but to identify problems, choose the hypothesis which is most fruitful, and choose the consequences which are most desirable. The task is not to complicate issues, but to reduce them to significant proportions definable by science, solvable by scientific methods, and capable of the scientific verification of others who repeat the process.

Since new problems emerge in an environment because of our lack of foresight and because past solutions may have created a new dilemma—like smog—the task of the pragmatist is never done. He must sell science to the public as the only way to avoid the problems —mostly pseudo—created by other philosophers, schools of thought, or artists who react to the world rather than work for meaningful ways of changing meaningful problematic situations which are real into meaningful plans for applying scientific procedures for resolving them. Since there is no end to nonsense until others learn to describe real problems scientifically, solve them scientifically, and weigh the consequences of their activities solely as the scientists weighs, measures, and verifies his investigations, the pragmatist, working primarily from a respect for science, will be kept very busy. One day his job may be made easier because the public will gradually learn to see the world solely as a place of real problems to be scientifically diagnosed, scientifically altered, and scientifically made less hectic.

What may appear to be other kinds of questions about morality and art which attempt to rank the behavior of men and the aesthetic pleasures cannot be ranked qualitatively or left to a different system of measurement. Even moral and aesthetic questions are really only scientific problems to be described, analyzed, and settled by the orderly and systematic application of scientific modes of investigation so that such values can be assigned a quantitative weight. Once these things are done, the world will come to more resemble a Utopia and less a Limbo where men ask foolish questions, lead confused lives, and multiply their problems. That such a day can come closer to realization is the faith of the pragmatist. In the meantime, he will continue to work to convince others that education and teaching and art, for example, can ultimately be scientifically understood and a plan for training teachers to educate the young according to the proven mode or program can be formulated. When this happens, there will be less waste and inefficiency in human activity and men will live less frightened and troubled existential lives. When such a day comes, there will be no Civil War in Northern Ireland and no Mideast Powder Keg.

The existentialist reviews all of the questions and all of the answers prior educational philosophers have proposed. He can understand that each philosophy has a set of assumptions and a rationale for viewing the education of man in and for the world. Just as he says, "They are all valid if . . . ," he says they are all also oversimplifications and incomplete and none of them could be completely realized without doing great harm to man. No single view has told the whole story—including existentialism. The world is likely to remain a place where all of the philosophies are practiced somewhere, by someone depending upon his culture, his many educational experiences, his place in historical time, and his autobiography. To dream that one philosophical view will come to be the only one would be more a tragedy than a victory. The amazing complexity of man and his many moods and responses to life are a source of wonderment and despair, and comedy and tragedy, to the existentialist. It may be that none of the primary assumptions of any of the philosophies is either totally true or totally false. Certainly, all yield results which their adherents value to be good and true for them. Indeed, it may be foolish to suppose that much of human value for all men can come from working from only one point of view or arriving at the proper goal. To set goals is inevitable, but no goal guarantees its own realization or worth. Confronted by the high drama of such a human condition and the complexity and variety of man's needs, the existentialist proposes to help man identify his many needs and find ways of coping with the variety of his problems, using a variety of methods and philosophies. In his view, the flavor and zest and all that makes life meaningful and meaningless would be lost if men tried to oversimplify the inevitable and exciting variety of beliefs, methods, and life-styles of men on earth.

For one group of philosophers to realize their single-minded goal and create their version of Utopia is to create a hell on earth for others with different needs, since all of the other systems are ultimately intolerant. Without assured guidelines and direction or foolproof methods of investigation, the world is still a challenging place where men can, perhaps, only survive if there is no one true way and all men subscribe to only one set of values. Such a world as the existentialists describe may not be the most secure place in the universe; but it is a place where a variety of men can live in the agony and ecstasy of making choices which give their lives human meaning, freedom, and dignity. Such a view is the ultimate in relativism, pluralism, and tolerance. Ironically, this latest system is a denial of systems and suggests only that we describe and understand and use all or none of the philosophies of education because the future is still a question mark. Men will define themselves by the choices they dare to make and cannot, as men, avoid making; for man forever creates and re-creates his own universe and the rules and frames of reference and systems by which he must judge himself—but not other men; for he has finally learned that to kill other men for not worshiping his gods is to compel them to kill him for not worshiping their gods. Surely the world is at last big enough and wise enough for many different men and their many different gods. This is the faith of the humanistic existentialist heretic who creates no new secular or sacred gods so that other men and other gods may live productively in harmony and mutual respect. They suggest not just that men be educated to fit into existing patterns of social, political, and economic organization, but that we consider reassessing the patterns to fit the dazzling complexity of human needs and life-styles so that human resources are not callously ignored or wantonly destroyed.

Though each of the philosophies introduced in this book is currently practiced by teachers who may not have been aware of the assumptions or world view from which they operate, the value of this invitation to learning is in the questions it poses rather than in any answers it may provide. For the teacher to function effectively as a unique individual as well as a member of a dedicated team devoted to the education of students, he must understand himself and regard his style of teaching critically and humbly: He owes his fellow teachers respect for how they choose to operate and why. Once the climate of candor, openness, and mutual respect is accepted, communication and meaningful dialog can begin to occur. Just as every philosophy has its great strengths, it also has its great dangers if carried to extremes or is accepted uncritically without regard for the checks and balances provided by each of the other philosophies with its strengths and weaknesses.

Let us, then, dispense with the dangerous illusion that the teacher's philosophy of education is different and apart from his less formal philosophy of life or that it is some form of scholastic anagrams to be endured for certification purposes. As teachers, what we do in the classroom cannot be separated from our attitudes about the purposes of education, the role of the teacher, ideas about the good life, and our beliefs about people as learners. More abstractly, we carry into the classroom convictions about the world, its meaning or absence of it, and our perceptions about how and why men relate to one another in specific societies and for what purposes. The teacher, beginner or veteran, cannot afford to be so apathetic or unthinking that this sense of priorities varies without purpose from setting to setting. If the teacher does not think about the rationale for his behavior as a trusted professional and how it affects others, he cannot hope to be effective in his dealings with others. Something more than drifting with the currents is called for.

Teaching is inevitably a moral and value-laden enterprise which takes place in an extremely complex social arena in which different groups hold competing if not contradictory values and expectations for the schools. Certainly, philosophy cannot operate in a vacuum of theory indifferent to developments in psychology, sociology, educational technology, and the issues and trends of the contemporary secular society. Though the school is a place which responds as adequately as possible to the many different kinds of demands made upon it, it is, at present, impossible for it to function effectively and be all things to all people — nor, perhaps should one school try lest it do nothing well. Nor is teaching a license to "do one's own thing" regardless of its consequences to others. The school is also entrusted with preparing students to function in a future different from the past and the present, and therefore controversy cannot be avoided about what are indeed the issues and trends which will affect how the schools operate and the courses they offer. The teacher is still the most vital and vulnerable participant in the educative process; whatever happens, he will literally be "in the middle of it." He is at once educator as well as thinker, role model, counselor, and participant; consequently, he must forever reassess what he does and why, and this is not easy. Knowing the options available to him and the rationales for them provided by the philosophies of education may help him "get it all together" so he can function and organize efficiently when he knows himself and what is possible for him.

He is an employee of a system and expected to operate within the framework and structure of the employing agency which is accountable to the publics which tax themselves to support it. If students in our mobile society transfer to a different school, they are expected to be able to perform at grade level. What range of curricular reform or resistance to it occurs is responsible not only to standardized tests used nationally, but is also boundaried by the specific departmental, educational, and regional expectations of the citizenry. Inevitably, the teacher is sensitized, but hopefully not paralyzed, by the awareness of what are often the conflicting expectations of him as teacher held by administrators, other teachers, students, and their parents. The teacher does inevitably personify some of these tensions in his dealings with his administration, colleagues, students, and neighbors. Consequently, he cannot afford to oversimplify the problems or forever retreat into theoretical or ivory tower justifications for his decisions as an excuse for his insensitivity to his professional and social responsibilities.

This means that the teacher in his behaviors is forever compelled not only to assess, but to reassess his ideas about his functions and relationships especially to students. The teacher is on the "front line" where the "action is" and his experiences with students are the real laboratory test of the efficacy of any philosophy of education. He may discover by being aware of the philosophies of education that no single one of them is a complete recipe book for solving all his problems and, indeed, that too zealous an adherence to any one of them will impair his functionings in the variety of settings in which he operates. The philosophies, then, are not programmed answers to every legitimate question; and they do not dispense instant solutions to complex problems. Knowing this, the teacher is equipped to think and rethink his problems as he must to be effective.

In a given class in mathematics, for example, the teacher may have an extremely bright student who does well in manipulating the symbols and performing the operations required of him with delight and success. Yet in the next seat may be a student who cannot understand mathematics who does very well — unlike the first student — in manipulating the abstractions of language or artistic expression. Some indifferent or average students may feel that the course is simply a required hurdle to college admission or that they don't need it and won't ever use it. Even with ability groupings there is bound to be a wide range of intellectual ability, social values, psychological and social needs, and behaviors exhibited among the students. The idealistic philosophy, for example, of meeting absolute, preset academic standards and training the intellect, if implemented in such a setting, would perhaps be appropriate for only a fraction of the students. What then, have we done, not *for,* but *to* the others? Different examples could illustrate the same hazard of indiscriminately applying any one of the other philosophies to the variety of complex classroom situations.

If the same teacher, as is very possible, teaches a course in introduction to public speaking during the next period, he may find himself operating under the different rationale of socializing the child for his cooperative life rather than refining a specialized skill which will make him more competitive. Has the role of the teacher not also to change as he moves from one period of the day to the next? In each case, he has as many responsibilities, trusts, and problems as he has students. Can he function in such different settings if his expectations for students and methods of working with them are constant? Is it possible that knowing how to use the philosophies effectively to choose among the rationales most appropriate for managing different courses and different students within the courses is ultimately more sane and helpful than evading the kinds of problems just identified by easy recourse to a favorite theory which rationalizes unthinking or instinctive teacher habitual behavior when innovation, open-mindedness, experimentation, and adventurous risk taking are called for?

Ultimately, the successful teacher comes to realize that most important issues in education from busing, to how schools are financed, to how students are grouped in what classes, to course offerings, to curricular reform, and to forms of grading and grading expectations, for example, are all essential *practical and philosophical problems.* Theory, then, does have a practical bearing on what happens in our schools and why; and it is the classroom teacher who copes with the many forces and pressures related to the teaching of the young. In his practice, the teacher not only assesses the reliability of current philosophies, but also refines the problems to be considered by future philosophies of education. A school, then, cannot call in a philosopher of education to fix everything that needs repair as if he were a mechanic repairing the heating system. Besides even if a specific school of philosophers claimed to be able to make piecemeal repairs of specific or recurrent breakdowns *after* they had occurred, no problems would be solved. Our preoccupations with process are well and good, but we are also responsible for the product of the processes. To forever replace valves or sections of pipe without regard for the effectiveness or complexity of the whole heating system is to deny the responsibility for what happens when the boiler bursts or the furnace explodes.

It is in the setting of the schools that the teacher serves as catalyst for helping to identify the priorities of education and ultimately evaluating the means of realizing them. To ignore theory, even though unrelated facts, and scores, and statistics are carefully assembled, is of little value except as a record of our failure to assess what is done; it is merely compulsive busywork and window dressing. To ignore the complex educational setting in which teaching and learning take place out of regard for some established philosophy of education is fatal to teaching and learning, and the educative process. Teachers and their experiences with students in the complex environment described must be more carefully considered by educational theorists, who are too often ignorant of the necessary complexity of the situation they attempt to direct. It is for these reasons that the teacher also has an obligation to influence theory makers rather than be only a passive implementer of some new pied piper who claims to have found the answer or the magic process for resolving all conflicts.

If we, as teachers, close off the great dialog about the philosophical problems of teaching effectively in the schools, fact and reliable theory will part company for good; and we, as teachers, will be the worse for it. If we are committed to improving the schools by our presence and to democracy as the embodiment of an ideal about the intelligence and trustworthiness of the citizenry to make their priorities known, we can suppose that the schools will continue to be a reflection of the values, or lack of them, of the greater society; we can also suppose that the priorities and values, or lack of them, we observe in society are partly an effect of what has been taught and learned in the schools. If a society disintegrates, no small part of the blame is the consequence of the failure of the schools. As teachers we must therefore be well informed and understand how our study of the problems addressed by the philosophies of education can animate our inquiry and suggest our subsequent actions. No philosophy should go unquestioned or be taken to be holy because it is either long-established or new. To suppose that all the important thinking about education has already been done by ivory tower specialists is to default — to "cop out" — and we have only ourselves as teachers to blame for what happens in the schools. For if we do nothing that too is a crude philosophy of sorts with disastrous results. As teachers on the battle line, we cannot close off the great debate about education out of deference to professional philosophers of education who teach only graduate-student research seminar courses. This is not the level where the problems of teachers of young people are confronted daily in an entirely different and more complex and hazardous environment. The classroom teacher then cannot oversimplify the problems by reducing their range, variety, and complexity or solve any of the practical philosophical problems of teaching effectively by understanding everything in abstract theory and accomplishing nothing in fact.

It is the teacher as moderator and carefully trained thinking professional who largely determines the relationships which will prevail between educational theory, educational practice, and how education is viewed in the society. As of now, some doubt understandably whether or not there are any remaining interrelationships. What we observe far more often, tragically, is a widening gap between the values of educational theorists, the teachers in the schools, and the rest of society. For the teacher to be apathetic or indifferent to the thoughts of the educational theorists or totally dependent upon them are equally disillusioned responses with equally harmful consequences. The teacher functions also in relationships to the range of values, expectations, and aspirations of groups within the society; and to ignore this interdependence is also to demolish what nervous confidence the public still has in our schools and its teachers.

To the end of providing at least a minimum of information and a list of helpful books and ways of thinking about educational philosophy for all those who may be interested in the topic, this capsule presentation of the basic concepts of educational philosophy is dedicated. If the book makes clear the need for continuing the study and debate about the purpose or purposes the schools serve and what citizens expect from students and teachers in their schools, the book has achieved its objective of opening rather than closing our perspectives about the teacher and his philosophy.

Glossary of Terms

This glossary of terms is intended to define some of the terms in the book with which you might have difficulty. It is neither elaborate nor complete. For a more complete and thorough listing, see Dagobert D. Runes (ed.), *Dictionary of Philosophy* (Ames, Iowa: New Student Outline Series; Littlefield, Adams & Co., 1959).

A Posteriori

Knowledge and principles derived from or dependent upon experience — inductive data gathering.

A Priori

Knowledge and principles of thinking that are *not* derived from experience and cannot be explained by experience.

Aesthetics

The study of what constitutes beauty and the foundations or assumptions upon which the assessment is based.

Analytic Thought

Unlike much speculative thought, analytic thought is carefully conducted critical investigation into the refinement of concepts and principles.

Axiology

An investigation into the source and warrant for discussions about what constitutes value and the basis for value judgments within the several major categories of philosophy.

Categorical Imperative

A set of statements by Kant of what ought to be done regardless of motive or consequence because it is always right.

Critical Realism

The notion that the material world external to the knower can be understood indirectly by way of mental constructs or psychological insights.

Deduction

The process of arriving logically at a conclusion from the consideration of several propositions—without denying or affirming the truth of the basic proposition.

Deontology

An assessment primarily of action derived totally from first principles, motive, or conscience independently of consequences.

Dualism

In its broadest use means reducing a wide variety of subject matter in any field of investigation to *two* irreducible principles—all human behavior is "good or evil"—all phenomena are "natural or supernatural."

Eclecticism

The knowing of ideas with various degrees of discrimination and systemization from more than one source of authority. For example, the eclectic in religion might develop what he hopes are the best concepts from all of the major world religions.

Epistemology

Broadly or loosely construed means "the theory of knowledge" or the study of "knowing"—the possibilities and limitations of knowing.

Essentialism

A philosophical position held by educators which mediates between the realist and idealistic extremes. Some essentials, like the three R's, resting on established knowledge and tradition must continue to be taught as the indisputable core of curriculum.

Ethics

An attempt to assess the morality of choices and an attempt to define criteria for defining what ought to be done in conduct in reference to broad categories like good and evil.

Existentialism

A modern philosophy which states that there are no reliable antecedent principles or values immune from criticism. It is by choice that values are acted out and therefore created or reaffirmed.

Experimentalism

A modern philosophy evolved from pragmatism which stresses the unique context of each problem and its refinement and possible solutions as projected by the intellectual model of scientific thinking.

Gestalt

Primarily a movement in European psychology more broadly and philosophically based than, for example, the limited categories of Freudian principles.

Idealism

Though there are degrees of idealism and several definitions, it generally means actions which attempt to approximate some preexistent ideal of right conduct.

Induction

Induction attempts to work from specific experiences to generalizations which are true of more than the sum total of unique instances; for example, we might generalize by induction that all rattlesnakes are poisonous.

Instrumentalism

A doctrine that the mind and ideas are instruments to aid individuals and groups in the solution of "real" problems not originating in the mind, but in the brute world of taxes and death.

Linguistic Analysis

A careful analytic study of the ways in which words are actually used within a context in the hope that the real problems can be uncovered and disputes which are merely verbal disposed of.

Logic

The careful study of what constitutes responsible thinking free of inconsistency, contradiction, or faulty causation considered within a coherent, theoretical frame of reference.

Logical Analysis

The scrupulous assessment of various claims to knowledge to determine their coherence and validity or truth as determined by the rules of logic and/or evidence within a specific context.

Logical Positivism

Sometimes called scientific empiricism. Based on the rigors of scientific thought, the logical positivists seek to verify knowledge scientifically by precise measurement; they also seek to relate words used as symbols to the objects or realities they signify.

Mentalism

An extreme of intellectualism which presupposes that relationships and concepts for organization exist almost solely within the minds rather than in the common-sense world.

Metaphysics

The study of conceptions or first principles beyond physical experience and not readily amenable to scientific verification or refutation.

Monism

The view that all the stuff of the world is of one irreducible substance — like atoms, for example — which underlies apparently different things like mind and matter.

New Realism

Primarily a reaction to the extremes of the idealistic position, the new realists attempt to understand the world "out there" which does operate in harmony with preestablished mental constructs, yet the external world can be understood directly by patient observers.

Ontology

Closely related to metaphysics, which is one aspect of it, ontology is the qualitative description of the hierarchy of layers of reality. Often based on the findings of science, it nevertheless speculates about the underlying principles of existence and attempts to record the implications of the varying interpretations and assumptions of differing world views.

Perennialism

Most often used by philosophies of education attempting to rationalize religious instruction, most notably neo-Thomism, perennialists try to reconcile the findings of science with the faith of the believer based also on revelation, authority, and dogma.

Philosophy

Broadly conceived, philosophy is the love of wisdom and the relentless inquiring after truth. As such, it attempts to enable men to seek consistently and coherently after the illusive integration and wholeness of self, society, and the world in a meaningful pattern.

Pluralism

A view which holds that the world is not made of one comprehensive substance (monism) or even two (dualism), but a variety of different and incompatible organizing principles all necessary to explain the complex flux and change of the mystifying world shared by all.

Pragmatism

An American philosophical movement which is a radical rejection of traditional philosophy, resting on the assumptions that the world of experience accessible to scientific inquiry is all we can know and that propositions and acts have meaning only in terms of their verifiable, public consequences.

Radical Empiricism

An extremely rigorous analytical position suspicious of broad generalizations however derived, usually limiting itself to a specific context and the uniqueness of situations which cannot be easily reduced into glib generalizations about other experiences with only superficial similarities.

Rationalism

Closely allied to deduction and a priori forms of thought, the rationalist holds that all important knowledge derives from reason and thought rather than sense experience and careful scientific inquiry.

Realism

The philosophical position that holds that the real world exists independently of any experience of it. Consequently, propositions are true only if they correspond with the known facts, laws, and principles of the objective world external to us.

Reconstructionism

An attempt in educational philosophy to deal with the crisis of transition by using education to enable individuals and groups to meet conceptualized goals and ends—like a clean environment—through the formalized educational structures.

Relativism

The ancient philosophical position given fresh credence by physics and cultural anthropology which stresses that creeds and codes are not and cannot be superficially assessed by reference to broad categories like good and evil; that is, different tribes and societies operate in accordance with their own socialized formulation of totems and taboos which are valid only in reference to themselves.

Solipsism

An extreme of mentalism closely related to idealism which holds that the self is entrapped within its own mental constructs which distort as much as support the phenomena of the external world. Such a view borders dangerously close to irrationalism.

Teleology

A branch of speculative philosophy which attempts to explain and evaluate present phenomena in terms of desired future consequences. Such a mind set presupposes man's rationality to comprehend the ultimate order and purpose operating in the universe.